CALIFORNIA

LEGAL HISTORY MANUSCRIPTS

IN THE HUNTINGTON LIBRARY

CALIFORNIA LEGAL HISTORY MANUSCRIPTS IN THE HUNTINGTON LIBRARY: A GUIDE

By

The Committee on History of Law in California
of The State Bar of California

Published by the
Henry E. Huntington Library and Art Gallery
San Marino, California
1989

Library of Congress Card Number 89-2167
ISBN 0-87328-099-7
Printed in the United States of America

Library of Congress Cataloging-in-Publication Data

Henry E. Huntington Library and Art Gallery.
California legal history manuscripts in the Huntington Library: a guide / by the Committee on History of Law in California of the State Bar of California.

1. Law – California – Manuscripts – Catalogs. 2. Law – California – History – Sources – Bibliography – Catalogs. 3. Manuscripts – California – San Marino – Catalogs. 4. Henry E. Huntington Library and Art Gallery – Catalogs.
I. State Bar of California. Committee on the History of Law in California.
II. Title.
KFC1.H46 1989
016.349794 –dc20 89-2167
[016.34794]

CONTRIBUTORS

The Committee on History of Law in California is pleased to acknowledge financial contributions from the following individuals, firms, and foundations to support the creation of this guide:

Allan L. Alexander, Esq., Los Angeles
American Bar Association, Chicago
The Durfee Foundation, San Diego
The Furth Foundation, San Francisco
James C. Greene, Esq., Los Angeles
Richard Guggenhime, Esq., San Francisco
The Huntington Library, San Marino
Kadison, Pfaelzer, Woodard, Quinn & Rossi, Los Angeles
McCutchen, Doyle, Brown & Enerson, San Francisco
Montgomery, Gascou, Gemmill & Thornton, Los Angeles
O'Melveny & Meyers, Los Angeles
John Salvatore Parise, Esq., Villa Park
Bernard Petrie, Esq., San Francisco
Pillsbury, Madison & Sutro, San Francisco
Tobin & Tobin, San Francisco
Troy & Casden, Los Angeles
Sidley & Austin, Los Angeles
Gibson, Dunn & Crutcher, Los Angeles

CONTENTS

PREFACE

This manuscript resource guide is a project of The Committee on History of Law in California, a standing committee of The State Bar of California. This work has two general purposes. First, it is a guide to certain manuscript resources at the Huntington Library in San Marino, California. The Huntington may be best known for its extensive gardens and treasured art museum, but it also houses one of the finest collections of rare books and archival manuscripts in the United States. Second, we hope that this guide sets an example of one possibility for improved access to manuscripts. This guide should also draw attention to the value of archives for legal history research. Our committee has found that many historians often overlook legal developments in their research, and we found that archivists and manuscript librarians seldom recognize the value of collections for the pursuit of legal history. This guide's most important innovation, however, is that it enables researchers to locate individual documents according to their subject. We hope it stimulates other archivists and librarians to see it as a model, and to develop other similar guides for legal historians.

In 1984, our committee chose to pursue a dual challenge. We wanted to develop subject access to manuscript collections from a legal perspective, and we wanted to facilitate a deeper understanding of legal history in archives and manuscript libraries. Our decision to conduct the project at the Huntington Library was relatively easy. Scholars from around the world have used the Huntington collections. Notable among those scholars is John Phillip Reid, a professor of law at New

York University. Professor Reid spends much of each year at the Huntington, and from his study he has written extensively on California legal history.[1] When we initially proposed this project, we received immediate support from Professor Reid and from Dr. Martin Ridge, Head of Research at the Huntington. Dr. Ridge made all the special arrangements for using the collections, and he obtained partial funding for this project from the Huntington's research grant funds. He also arranged permission for us to base the general collection descriptions in this guide on descriptions already published by the Huntington.[2]

The committee retained the services of Gordon Morris Bakken, professor of history at California State University, Fullerton, to compile the information for the guide. Professor Bakken has written extensively on California legal history.[3] He has based much of his research during the past fifteen years at the Huntington. Bakken is a product of the "Willard Hurst" school of legal history; he earned his doctorate and his law degree at the University of Wisconsin, where Professor Hurst has been a leading force in American legal history. We were fortunate to have had the talented and untiring services of Professor Bakken throughout this project. We were also fortunate to have the efforts of someone already familiar with the Huntington collections. He brought to the task an understanding of the scholar's concerns and methods. Virtually all of this guide's format and contents were shaped by Bakken's scholarship and interests. Perhaps that fact reveals an element of subjectivity in the creation of subject access to archives, but we believe that the resulting product will be useful to all legal historians, regardless of their particular interests or philosophies.

The Committee on History of Law in California has a full agenda, and committee members are generally responsible for planning and carrying out all of the committee's projects. This guide, however, marks the first time that the committee has retained outside services to pursue a job. Because the committee's funds from The State Bar are limited to administrative expenses, we had to embark on extensive fundraising to begin and complete this guide. Three San Francisco law firms generously provided assistance in preparing our hundreds of solicitation letters: Canterbury, Raub & Greenthal; Cooley, Godward, Castro, Huddleston & Tatum; and Knox & Cincotta.

After more than a year of letters and grant applications, we received the necessary funds, and we are pleased to acknowledge support from the lawyers, law firms, and foundations listed at the beginning of this publication. Their contributions demonstrate the importance of this project to scholars and to the community of California attorneys. We thank them for making this guide possible. Their contributions proved that subject access to archives can overcome the barrier of anticipated costs.[4]

We received support and assistance from many individuals at various stages of working on this guide. We thank many members of the Huntington staff, in addition to Dr. Ridge, who gave critical support. Robert Middlekauff, former Director of the Huntington, endorsed this project, and several of the manuscript curators, particularly Mary Robertson, Virginia Rust, and William P. Frank, gave important assistance and advice. In Professor Bakken's office in Fullerton, we thank his secretary, Barbara McDowell, who prepared numerous drafts of this work. We also thank Professor Bakken himself for accepting this challenge. He worked patiently and productively with a committee of critics reviewing his drafts and offering a wide range of comments. Committee members generously pored over many versions of this guide, and all shared the objective of creating a product that can be both useful and innovative. In particular three Committee chairpersons—Christian G. Fritz, Kenneth D. Crews, and Laurene Wu McClain—undertook the task of editing and completing the guide. Committee member Neil T. Gotanda and his colleague Philip Merkel also assisted greatly in that final process. Finally we thank Margaret F. Carter who typed accurately and efficiently several drafts of this guide.

We hope that users of this work will share their comments with us. We hope that experience now will lead to improved projects in the future. We also hope that organizations and institutions elsewhere will be inspired to develop other means of providing access to manuscript collections, and that they will test and implement those finding aids for the benefit of scholars and researchers everywhere.

THE COMMITTEE ON HISTORY OF LAW IN CALIFORNIA

Rosalyn S. Zakheim, Chair, 1988-1989
John K. Hanft, Chair, 1987-1988
Laurene Wu McClain, Chair, 1986-1987
Kenneth D. Crews, Chair, 1985-1986
Christian G. Fritz, Chair, 1984-1985
Eric A. Chiappinelli, Chair, 1983-1984

NOTES

1 For one of his recent publications drawing on the Huntington collections, see John Phillip Reid, *Law for the Elephant: Property and Social Behavior on the Overland Trail* (San Marino: Huntington Library, 1980).

2 The previously published descriptions appear in *Guide to American Historical Manuscripts in the Huntington Library* (San Marino: Huntington Library, 1979).

3 One of his most recent publications is *The Development of Law on Frontier California: Civil Law and Society, 1850-1890* (Westport, Conn.: Greenwood Press, 1985).

4 For an example of financial concerns as a barrier, see Richard C. Berner, "Arrangement and Description of Manuscripts," *Drexel Library Quarterly* 11 (January 1975): 51.

INTRODUCTION

The Huntington Library in San Marino, California is rich in manuscript collections, and many of them are valuable in the study of California legal history. This guide will direct scholars, lawyers, and other researchers to those collections and to specific items within the collections. The guide itself has two main parts, each supporting a very different approach to historical research. The first part is the "Subject Access Guide." The Subject Access Guide is essentially a subject index to relevant manuscript materials at the Huntington. Its objective is to lead researchers to individual documents and to sets of documents by their subject. The second part of the guide is a description of collections of interest to legal historians. That part assesses the significance of each collection for research purposes. The documents analyzed in the Subject Access Guide are from the collections described in the latter part of this work.

The methodology for creating this guide was ostensibly simple, but very time-consuming. The effort to create this work, however, is intended to reduce the research time for later historians employing it at the Huntington. First, the State Bar Committee, the Huntington professional staff, and I identified collections with significant or unusual potential for legal history research. Nearly every Huntington collection contains documents of interest to legal history, but we attempted to limit our study to collections directly related to the law or with peculiar or substantial holdings. Researchers should consult the Huntington's professional staff regarding any collections not included here that may also be useful for any related research. For example, two very interesting collections, the Henry Edwards Huntington Collection and the Frank Latta Collection, are not included in this guide, because they are not specifically law-related. Each collection, however, contains real estate and business papers of potential interest.

Second, I studied each collection to locate materials with legal history implications. I identified within each such item a broad field of law to which it related: contracts, labor, taxation, or other area. Those areas became the subject headings in the Subject Access Guide. My objective at this stage was to anticipate the general topic a researcher wanting the particular document may be pursuing. I added more specific subdivisions whenever appropriate. The Subject Access Guide which follows arranges the identified documents under their designated subject heading, thereby allowing subject access to the Huntington collections. To use the Subject Access Guide effectively, the researcher should have a general idea of the subject matter of interest. The Huntington collections which deal with California law are predominantly from the nineteenth century and involve real estate, agriculture, and industries such as mining, oil, and commerce. For the lawyer of the period, these areas of activity generated a large property and contract law business. Property law practice involved the acquisition, development, use, and transfer of real estate. Contract practice pertained to the transactions of a dynamic era of entrepreneurialism in the nineteenth century. It continued into the maturing industrial economy of twentieth-century California.

This guide's second section contains a general description of each collection and assesses its probable usefulness for legal history research. I have labeled as "significant" those collections containing numerous documents of legal history import. Collections with fewer documents or standard legal forms only are labeled "moderately significant." Collections with few, scattered, or only general form documents without substantial collateral correspondence are labeled "marginal."

These evaluations allow researchers to locate useful collections and documents quickly. The significant and moderately significant collections are critical to a full understanding of legal history in California.

Although this work can guide users to the Huntington's important collections and documents in the study of California legal history, researchers must note that this guide has inherent limitations: the collections and documents referred to here are selective. First, the guide includes those collections that are fully cataloged. When the Huntington catalogs a collection, a card for every piece in the collection is entered into a manuscript catalog, much like the familiar card catalog used for books in most libraries. The catalog enables easy reference to the nature of the document, the parties named in the document, the date, and collection location. I used the manuscript catalog extensively in the preparation of this guide. However, it also includes those collections denoted as "rough sorted" or "semi-cataloged." The "rough sorted" or "semi-cataloged" collections do not have every piece itemized in the manuscript catalog. The collections are, however, physically arranged for research purposes. Some of these collections have correspondence arranged in chronological order with other types of documents sorted in separate boxes. Other such collections have documents arranged by topic. Research in these collections requires an item-by-item perusal. The Huntington intends eventually to process some of these collections more fully. Researchers should consult the Huntington for the current cataloging status of a collection. In particular, the Fletcher Bowron, John Anson Ford, Jackson Alpheus Graves, Thomas R. Bard, and David Jacks collections are "semi-cataloged" at this time. The Huntington may complete the cataloging of these and other collections in the coming years, and more complete cataloging will obviously ease research.

Entries in the Subject Access Guide are also selective. For collections such as the papers of Jackson Alpheus Graves and other attorneys, virtually all of the documents are worthy of consideration by legal historians. This guide identifies only those documents that are most interesting or relevant in the legal history inquiry. This guide may therefore unduly focus attention on individual items or collections, but researchers should not simply review the materials in isolation.

The procedure for using this guide is very simple, but can involve many subtleties. The researcher exploring a legal history topic should consult both parts of this guide. First, the Subject Access Guide lists documents individually or in related sets under appropriate subject headings. For each document listed, the guide also provides the document's collection, the box number where stored, the document's date, and a note about the nature or character of the document. Second, each collection description in the second part of this guide lists all of the subject headings given to documents in the collection. That list aids the researcher in understanding the collection's breadth and general topics. It also indicates where more information about the collection may be found in the Subject Access Guide.

Once this guide has directed users to documents and collections of interest, those materials may be studied at the Huntington Library. The library does not loan or otherwise circulate any materials from the manuscript collections, but welcomes requests for further information and assists researchers by making photocopies of materials. Users of this guide should contact the Huntington for its policies regarding entry to the library and use of collections.

Locating documents is based on the notes in the last column of the Subject Access Guide. Cataloged collections at the Huntington have a separate folder for each item, and the "Finder's Aid" column is based on the individual folder labels. For example, if the Finder's Aid states "Alfred A. Jones to James de Barth Shorb," the researcher can review the alphabetically arranged manuscript folders in the box until finding "Alfred A. Jones" on the left margin of the manuscript folder. That folder contains the document referred to in this guide. If the description in this guide is "Alfred A. Jones to

Shorb, various," the researcher should review all of the "Alfred A. Jones" documents that also reference "James de Barth Shorb" on the folder's right margin. If the description is "Alfred A. Jones to various," all of the "Alfred A. Jones" documents in that box will be relevant. Any dates noted in the Subject Access Guide may limit the search among multiple folders.

I hope that users will find this guide to be both helpful and accurate and will contact either me or the Huntington staff with any queries or suggestions for improvement for this or future guides.

Gordon Morris Bakken
California State University, Fullerton

USING THE SUBJECT ACCESS GUIDE

The Subject Access Guide is divided into alphabetical sections by subject heading, from "Admiralty" to "Water." The information on each document under a subject heading is then arranged in columns. The first column is a subdivision. Although not every item in the guide has a subdivision, the additional detail it provides can focus research. The subdivision is also not always a "subject." That is, the term is a subject when it clarifies what the item is "about." Sometimes, however, the term indicates the "form" of the item. For example, a subdivision "Bankruptcy" indicates what the document may be about. It tells something of its subject. On the other hand, a subdivision "deed" indicates that the document is itself a deed; it thus indicates the item's "form."[1] The choice of subdivision is based on the anticipated information that the researcher may need to best begin exploring his or her topic in the manuscript collections.

The second column names the collection to which the document belongs. The third column is the number of the box in that collection where the document is stored. The fourth column is the document's date. The final column, "Finder's Aid," gives details about the nature or character of the document. Those details will help the researcher to evaluate the document's significance and to locate it in the collection.

On pages 9 through 19 the subject headings used in the Subject Access Guide are listed with references to subdivisions and collections pertaining to the subject headings. On pages 21 through 25 the subdivisions are listed with reference to subject headings under which the subdivisions will appear in the Subject Access Guide. On pages 27 through 38 descriptions of subject headings used in the Subject Access Guide are provided.

[1] The problem of "subject" versus "form" is common in the effort to provide subject access to archives. According to one writer, "In the archive world one continually comes up against what I can only term the myth that, because archive material generally differs from books, their subject matter cannot be classified by the same system, that the subject matter of a document cannot be assigned to a subject class in the same way as a book's. This myth often co-exists with a confusion between content and physical form — deed, court roll, plan, letter, and so on." Steven L. Hensen, "The Use of Standards in the Application of the AMC Format," *American Archivist* 49 (Winter 1986): 38.

SUBJECT HEADINGS IN THE GUIDE

Subject Headings	*Subdivisions*	*Collections*
Admiralty	Bankruptcy	Catlin
		Fernald
		Graves
		Haight
		Halleck
		Leidesdorff
		Markham
Agriculture	Citrus Business	Azusa
	Fencing	Bacon
	Title	Center
	Wine Business	Crank
		Graves
		Jacks
		Keller
		Markham
		Shorb
		Wilson
		Wolfskill
Banking	Taxation	Adams & Co.
		Bacon
		Graves
Commercial Law	Bill of Exchange	Adams & Co.
	Brandy Trade	Baker
	Legal Tender	Center
	Promissory Note	El Dorado Cty.

Subject Headings	*Subdivisions*	*Collections*
Commercial Law (cont.)	Sales	Fernald
		Graves
		Haight
		Jones
		Keller
		Leidesdorff
		Markham
		Shorb
		Stearns
		Stimson
		Wilson
		Wolfskill
		Woodworth
Constitutional Law	Appointment	Baker
	Birth Control	Bowron
	Counties	Fernald
	Elections	Haight
	Sabbath	Mandeville
	Suffrage	Markham
		Park
		Shorb
		Stanton
Contracts	Breach	Adams & Co.
	Chattel Mortgage	Baker
	Creditors	Barclay
	Deed	Bard
	Employment	Bowron
	Lawyers	Center
	Railroad	Chipman
	Real Property	Couts
	Warranty	Crank
	Water	Fernald
		Graves
		Haight
		Heslop

Subject Headings	*Subdivisions*	*Collections*
Contracts (cont.)		Houghton
		Keller
		Leidesdorff
		Mandeville
		Markham
		McCullough
		Morgan
		O'Farrell
		Potter
		Russell
		Shorb
		Wolfskill
Corporations	Bonds	Azusa
	Mortgage	Baldwin
	Partnership	Barclay
	Taxation	Chipman
		Crank
		Fernald
		Graves
		Haight
		Keller
		Markham
		Morgan
		Potter
		Shorb
		Wolfskill
Crimes	Assault	Adams & Co.
	Battery	Aram
	Burglary	Baldwin
	Contract	Bowron
	Gambling	Brent
	Grand Jury	Dane
	Homicide	Fernald
	Horse Theft	Ford

Subject Headings	*Subdivisions*	*Collections*
Crimes (cont.)	Liquor	Graves
	Parole	Haight
	Petty Theft	Hoadley
	Prevention	Jacks
	Prostitution	Kincade
	Rape	Leidesdorff
	Sanity	Mandeville
		Morgan
		Park
		S. F. Comm.
		Terry
		Watkins
		Woolwine
Debtor and Creditor	Admiralty	Adams & Co.
	Attachment	Bacon
	Bankruptcy	Baker
	Deed	Baldwin
	Garnishment	Center
	Mechanic's Lien	Crank
		Fernald
		Graves
		Haight
		Halleck
		Mandeville
		Markham
		Morgan
		New Almaden
		Russell
		Shorb
		Terry
		Watkins
		Wolfskill
Environmental Law	Air Pollution	Bowron
		Ford
		Shorb

Subject Headings in the Guide

Subject Headings	*Subdivisions*	*Collections*
Estates	Banking	Baldwin
	Bankruptcy	Center
	Contract	Chipman
	Creditors	Couts
	Deed	Fernald
	Executor	Graves
	Guardianship	Haight
	Homestead	Jones
	Mortgage	Keller
	Probate	Leidesdorff
	Promissory Note	Markham
	Real Property	McCullough
	Taxation	New Almaden
	Trust	Shorb
	Will	Stanton
		Stimson
		Wilson
		Wolfskill
		Woodworth
Family Law	Community Property	Baldwin
	Divorce	Couts
		Haight
		Houghton
		Park
		Watkins
Insurance		Chipman
		Graves
		Markham
		Stanton
		Wolfskill
Labor	Arbitration	Aram
		Bowron
		Markham
		Park
		Shorb

Subject Headings	*Subdivisions*	*Collections*
Labor (cont.)		Watkins
Landlord & Tenant	Agriculture	Adams & Co.
	Hotel	Barclay
	Lease	Center
	Mining	Fernald
	Oil	Graves
	Promissory Note	Houghton
	Public Utilities	Howell
	Rent	Jacks
	Title	Keller
		Leidesdorff
		Markham
		Morgan
		O'Farrell
		Potter
		Price
		Shorb
		Wolfskill
Law & Practice	Courts	Adams & Co.
	Deed	Aram
	Fees	Bell
	Jurisprudence	Bowron
	Law Books	Burnett
	Lawyers	Center
	Litigation	Chipman
	Practice	Dalton
	Procedure	Dane
	Stat. of Lims.	El Dorado
	Venue	Fernald
		Graves
		Haight
		Halleck
		Jacks
		Jones

Subject Headings	***Subdivisions***	***Collections***
Law & Practice (cont.)		Leidesdorff
		Markham
		Shorb
		Stimson
		Terry
		Woolwine
Municipalities	Airports	Bowron
	Bonds	Center
	Recreation	Crank
	Roads	Fernald
	Zoning	Ford
		Graves
		Mandeville
		Markham
		Wilson
		Woolwine
Natural Resources	Mining	Aram
	Oil	Baker
	Promissory Note	Baldwin
		Bard
		Brophy-Beeson
		Center
		Chipman
		Couts
		Crank
		El Dorado
		Fernald
		Ford
		Graves
		Haight
		Hoadley
		Keller
		Kincade
		Mandeville
		Markham

Subject Headings	*Subdivisions*	*Collections*
Natural Resources (cont.)		Morgan
		New Almaden
		Potter
		Shorb
		Stimson
		Wolfskill
		Woodworth
Patent Law		Shorb
Public Utilities	Crimes	Graves
		Potter
Railroads	Contract	Crank
	Eminent Domain	Fernald
	Rates	Graves
	Real Property	Haight
		Jacks
		Markham
		Railroadiana
		Shorb
Real Property	Adverse Possession	Adams & Co.
	Attachment	Aram
	Bankruptcy	Azusa
	Bond	Bacon
	Boundaries	Baker
	Bounty Warrant	Baldwin
	Chinese Rights	Barclay
	Condemnation	Bard
	Contract	Bell
	Conveyance	Bowron
	Covenant	Brent
	Deed	Brophy-Beeson
	Ejectment	Catlin
	Eminent Domain	Center
	Mining	Chipman
	Mortgage	Couts
	Oil	Crank

Subject Headings	*Subdivisions*	*Collections*
Real Property (cont.)	Reconveyance	Dalton
	Recording	Dane
	Redemption	El Dorado
	Rescission	Fernald
	Sale	Graves
	Tax Titles	Haight
	Taxation	Halleck
	Title	Heslop
	Trespass	Hoadley
	Trust	Houghton
	Water	Howell
	Wine Business	Jacks
		Jones
		Keller
		Leidesdorff
		Mandeville
		Markham
		McCullough
		Morgan
		New Almaden
		O'Farrell
		Orange Cty.
		Potter
		Shorb
		Stearns
		Stimson
		Terry
		Wilson
		Wolfskill
		Wolter
		Woodworth
Taxation		Adams & Co.
		Baker
		Bowron
		Crank

Subject Headings	*Subdivisions*	*Collections*
Taxation (cont.)		El Dorado
		Fernald
		Ford
		Graves
		Haight
		Mandeville
		Morgan
		Shorb
		Stimson
		Terry
		Watkins
		Wolfskill
Title	Agriculture	Chipman
		Dalton
		Haight
		Halleck
		Jacks
		Jones
		Keller
		Leidesdorff
		McCullough
		Markham
		New Almaden
		O'Farrell
		Potter
		Price
		Stearns
		Wolter
Torts	Defamation	Bowron
	Insurance	Fernald
	Libel	Graves
	Railroads	Shorb
	Sovereign Immun.	
	Wrongful Death	

Subject Headings in the Guide

Subject Headings	***Subdivisions***	***Collections***
Water	Contract	Azusa
	Corporations	Barclay
	Deed	Bard
	Easement	Bowron
	Eminent Domain	Catlin
	Estate	Center
	Mortgage	Crank
	Pollution	Dalton
	Rates	Fernald
		Ford
		Graves
		Heslop
		Hoadley
		Keller
		Kincade
		Mandeville
		Markham
		Potter
		Shorb
		Wolfskill

SUBDIVISIONS IN THE GUIDE

Subdivisions	*Subject Headings*
Admiralty	Debtor & Creditor
Adverse Possession	Real Property
Agriculture	Landlord & Tenant
	Title
Air Pollution	Environmental Law
Airports	Municipalities
Apportionment	Constitutional Law
Arbitration	Labor
Assault	Crimes
Attachment	Debtor & Creditor
	Real Property
Banking	Estates
Bankruptcy	Admiralty
	Debtor & Creditor
	Estates
	Real Property
Battery	Crimes
Bill of Exchange	Commercial Law
Birth Control	Constitutional Law
Bonds	Corporations
	Municipalities
Boundaries	Real Property
Bounty Warrant	Real Property
Brandy Trade	Commercial Law
Breach	Contracts

Subdivisions	***Subject Headings***
Burglary	Crimes
Chattel Mortgage	Contracts
Chinese Rights	Real Property
Citrus Business	Agriculture
Community Property	Family Law
Condemnation	Real Property
Contract	Crimes
	Estates
	Railroads
	Real Property
	Water
Conveyance	Real Property
Corporations	Water
Counties	Constitutional Law
Courts	Law & Practice
Covenant	Real Property
Creditors	Contracts
	Estates
Deed	Contracts
	Debtor & Creditor
	Estates
	Law & Practice
	Real Property
	Water
Defamation	Torts
Divorce	Family Law
Easement	Water
Ejectment	Real Property
Eminent Domain	Railroads
	Real Property
	Water
Employment	Contracts

Subdivisions in the Guide

Subdivisions	*Subject Headings*
Estate	Water
Executor	Estates
Fees	Law & Practice
Fencing	Agriculture
Gambling	Crimes
Garnishment	Debtor & Creditor
Grand Jury	Crimes
Guardianship	Estates
Homestead	Estates
Horse Theft	Crimes
Hotel	Landlord & Tenant
Insurance	Torts
Jurisprudence	Law & Practice
Law Books	Law & Practice
Lawyers	Contracts
	Law & Practice
Lease	Landlord & Tenant
Legal Tender	Commercial Law
Libel	Torts
Liquor	Crimes
Litigation	Law & Practice
Mechanic's Lien	Debtor & Creditor
Mining	Landlord & Tenant
	Natural Resources
	Real Property
Mortgage	Corporations
	Estates

Subdivisions	***Subject Headings***
Mortgage (cont.)	Real Property
	Water
Oil	Landlord & Tenant
	Natural Resources
	Real Property
Parole	Crimes
Partnerships	Corporations
Petty Theft	Crimes
Pollution	Water
Practice	Law & Practice
Prevention	Crimes
Probate	Estates
Procedure	Law & Practice
Promissory Note	Commercial Law
	Estates
	Landlord & Tenant
	Natural Resources
Prostitution	Crimes
Public Utility	Landlord & Tenant
Railroad	Contracts
	Torts
Rape	Crimes
Rates	Railroads
	Water
Real Property	Contracts
	Estates
	Railroads
Reconveyance	Real Property
Recording	Real Property
Recreation	Municipalities
Redemption	Real Property
Rent	Landlord & Tenant

Subdivisions in the Guide

Subdivisions	*Subject Headings*
Rescission	Real Property
Roads	Municipalities
Sabbath	Constitutional Law
Sales	Commercial Law
	Real Property
Sanity	Crimes
Sovereign Immunity	Torts
Statute of Limitations	Law & Practice
Suffrage	Constitutional Law
Tax Titles	Real Property
Taxation	Banking
	Corporations
	Estates
	Real Property
Title	Agriculture
	Landlord & Tenant
	Real Property
Trespass	Real Property
Trust	Estates
	Real Property
Venue	Law & Practice
Warranty	Contracts
Water	Contracts
	Landlord & Tenant
	Real Property
Will	Estates
Wine Business	Agriculture
	Real Property
Wrongful Death	Torts
Zoning	Municipalities

DESCRIPTION OF SUBJECT HEADINGS

ADMIRALTY

Admiralty, the field of law dealing with the transportation of goods or passengers by water, forms an important chapter in California's legal history. Particularly in the wake of the Gold Rush, ships provided vital transportation, communication, and economic links between the isolated west coast and other parts of the world, especially the eastern states. Later, important trade developed across the Pacific, particularly between California and China. In addition, a vigorous nineteenth-century coastal trade using extensive inland waterways brought a host of other activities before the courts hearing admiralty matters.

Prior to the completion of the transcontinental railroad in 1869, admiralty litigation involving seaborne commerce provides one of the best pictures of the business community in San Francisco and commerce in the state generally. Moreover, in the suits brought by sailors for their wages or to rectify mistreatment they suffered, many insights can be gained into the condition and experience of shipboard life in the nineteenth century. Additionally, the numerous suits brought by disgruntled ship passengers before the federal district court in San Francisco reveal many of the hardships encountered by people who traveled to California by sea.

Finally, historians interested in changing conceptions of federalism will find much of interest in the struggles between state and federal courts over admiralty jurisdiction in California during the 1850s and 1860s.

AGRICULTURE

The origins and development of commercial agriculture in California are reflected in various collections at the Huntington Library. In particular, the emergence of the citrus business in Pasadena and in Southern California generally during the nineteenth and early twentieth centuries can be traced. A number of collections deal with early California wineries, especially in Southern California, and the growth of agricultural activity around Monterey and Santa Cruz. Apart from correspondence about the business and management practices, there are documents detailing occasional disputes over title to agricultural land and fencing.

BANKING

California's early express and banking firms played an important part in the economic development of the state. Several collections consist of the papers of individuals who owned or ran such firms and they reveal much about banking methods and the dynamics of business in the nineteenth and early twentieth centuries. In some cases these papers document precisely how banking institutions promoted economic growth and financed specific industries, especially the railroads. The volatile financial environment in which these early banks operated can be appreciated by their sometimes spectacular failures, particularly in the 1850s. A number of collections also contain information about several banks that went into receivership or encountered other legal problems.

COMMERCIAL LAW

This subject heading includes the legal dynamics of early commercial and business enterprises in the state to the extent that they are reflected in Huntington Library collections. The collections listed under this heading reveal much about the nature of doing business in the late nineteenth and early twentieth centuries in California. In several other related headings — including contracts and corporations — more detail can be gathered on the specific organization of business. The collections indexed under commercial law, however, offer a general perspective on a broad range of commercial activities including agriculture, banking, mining, and transportation.

CONSTITUTIONAL LAW

During the nineteenth century two constitutional conventions were held in California, the first in 1849 and the second in 1878-1879. Some of the collections in the Huntington Library shed light on the background of these conventions and controversies arising under the two constitutions. Much more than private legal disputes, constitutional issues tended to generate considerable public attention and political conflict. Issues such as observing the sabbath and women's suffrage, for example, developed constitutional dimensions. Moreover, discriminatory legislation directed at the Chinese in the nineteenth century and anti-Chinese sentiment formed an important undercurrent to the constitutional convention of 1878.

CONTRACTS

Contracts were and are important devices that define and regulate commercial transactions and business relationships. They figure prominently in collections that include materials dealing with businesses, land transactions, and other types of commercial activities. Documentary evidence of contracts tells much about business relationships and commercial activity. The documents themselves also shed light on the nature of legal practice and the level of legal sophistication of the lawyers who drew them up. As a result, the contracts in the Huntington's collections are important sources of California's legal history.

CORPORATIONS

The legal business structure of the corporation played a significant role in California's legal history. The corporate structure allowed capital investment on a large scale and some businesses, such as the railroads, developed enormous economic and political power. The public perception of the way railroads wielded their power in the late nineteenth century brought them under increasing scrutiny and criticism. Many other California businesses and industries became corporations, including the large-scale quartz mining operations of the 1860s and 1870s. Various Huntington collections contain information about corporate businesses and their leaders.

CRIMES

The maintenance of law and order has long been a staple theme of historians of the state. The extra-legal vigilance movements in San Francisco during the 1850s, in particular, have attracted attention. A variety of Huntington collections offer valuable insights into the Vigilance Committees of 1851 and 1856.

Because of their inherent drama, the vigilance movements have received a disproportionate share of historical interest. Perhaps even more significant are the references to criminal activity and the criminal law by lawyers who encountered these problems on a day-by-day basis. In many Huntington collections a more typical picture of crime and criminal prosecution emerges, including crimes against property (such as burglary, horse theft, petty theft) as well as against persons (such as assault, battery, homicide, and rape).

DEBTOR AND CREDITOR

This subject heading refers to the relationship between debtors and creditors as reflected in a variety of Huntington collections. Collections dealing with banking enterprises abound in documents that detail the extent and variety of indebtedness. Debtor/creditor relations not only reveal much about the business history of the state but the collection of debt also formed an important part of the legal practice of many lawyers.

ENVIRONMENTAL LAW

Several Huntington collections touch upon the desire to preserve the environment and efforts to use the law to obtain that objective. Under this subject heading the principal concerns reflected in some of the twentieth-century collections deal with air pollution. To a lesser extent the nineteenth-century collections also contain expressions of concern for the environment and tell of pressures to create natural preserves, most notably Yosemite National Park. For the most part, however, environmental concerns of the nineteenth century arose as a result of economic rather than aesthetic considerations.

ESTATES

This subject heading refers to the documentation and materials in a number of Huntington collections dealing with last will and testaments. Estate settlements provide a means not only of measuring the financial worth of a particular person but of assessing business practices. The various estate papers of the Cave Johnson Couts collection, for example, are useful summaries of late nineteenth- and early twentieth-century economic practices in California. Many of the estate papers reflect the business dealings of prominent Californians and reveal how great amounts of real property were disposed.

FAMILY LAW

Family law in the context of this guide refers to the legal relationships and responsibilities of family members. Included under this heading are materials and documents dealing with marriage and divorce. Numerous collections in the Huntington deal with these matters, including the implications of divorce given the doctrine of common property.

Apart from the legal aspects of the family, many collections contain information on the lives and legal status of women in the nineteenth and early twentieth centuries. Especially rich in this regard is the correspondence between men and their wives and families during and after the Gold Rush. Of particular interest is the Alice Locke Park collection, which offers insights into the life of the author and promoter of a California law adopted in 1913 that granted women equal rights of guardianship over their children.

INSURANCE

Some of the Huntington collections contain references to various forms of insurance used in the late nineteenth- and early twentieth-century California. Included under this heading are policies and correspondence relating to life, fire, and business insurance.

LABOR

Labor historians will be interested in the collections listed under this subject heading. The hiring of workers and labor relations can be studied in a number of collections, especially those relating to the nineteenth-century citrus business. The papers dealing with the operation of such businesses offer perspectives on labor relations that contrast with the papers of several California politicians who also dealt with such issues. The collections dealing with a former mayor of Los Angeles (Fletcher Bowron, 1938-1953) and former governor of California (Henry H. Markham, 1890-1895) are useful in this regard.

LANDLORD & TENANT

The relationship between landlord and tenant emerges in a wide variety of contexts in California's legal history and can be found in a substantial number of collections. Leases for dwellings, wharfs, agricultural lands, and mining and oil form only a partial list of the lease documents to be found at the Huntington. Many collections depict the affairs of large land holders who spent a great deal of their time (and that of the lawyers they hired) arranging for leases and collecting rents.

LAW & PRACTICE

This subject heading includes a wide range of activities of lawyers and judges specifically and the legal profession and the judicial system generally. A number of collections permit the reconstruction of legal practice in California during the late nineteenth and early twentieth centuries. Information about the lawyers themselves, the types of cases litigated, the costs of legal practice and fees received, and attitudes towards the judiciary are sprinkled throughout the collections. In addition, some collections present a fascinating picture of a succession of lawyers handling the legal affairs of large landowners, in which the client often became quite intrigued with the law and debated the merits of various types of legal action with his lawyer.

To the extent that the operation of state courts can be traced in personal correspondence, such material can be found under this subject heading. The most valuable source for the institutional history of California's judiciary, however, remains in county court records and state archives where a great deal of the work product of lawyers and the courts remains intact. The Huntington collections and other materials nicely complement these other records.

MUNICIPALITIES

Some of the Huntington's collections contain the papers of individuals who served as mayors of California cities or even as governors of the state. Such collections shed light on the variety of challenges and problems faced by city and state government in the nineteenth and twentieth centuries from the perspective of those intimately involved in government. The issues that emerge in the correspondence range from the construction of roads and airports to bond issues, zoning matters, and the creation of recreational areas.

NATURAL RESOURCES

The allocation of natural resources in California, particularly in the wake of the Gold Rush, forms one of the most important chapters of the state's legal history. Under this subject heading two other important natural resources, real property and water, are excluded and considered under their own subject headings. The collections listed under natural resources pertain mainly to the activities and legal struggles over mineral and oil extraction. Many collections are particularly rich in materials dealing with nineteenth-century gold mining, with the initial placer mining and the later large-scale quartz mining operations.

Also included under this heading are correspondence and materials dealing with the development of oil fields and oil production in Southern California.

PATENT LAW

Very few Huntington collections deal with the topic of patent law. In fact, most references under this subject heading come from the James de Barth Shorb collection and relate to his efforts to patent inventions dealing with agricultural equipment.

PUBLIC UTILITIES

Included under this subject heading are papers and materials dealing with the formation, operation, and litigation of early California water and electric companies. Most of the materials deal with utilities serving the southwestern portion of the United States. The Potter collection in particular contains valuable papers of a legal partnership that represented water and power companies in California during the early twentieth century.

RAILROADS

Railroads played a key role in California's history, particularly in the later part of the nineteenth century. After the transcontinental railroad linked California and the eastern United States in 1869, intra-state railroading increased dramatically. As the transportation system developed, railroads, particularly the Central Pacific, wielded enormous economic and political power. The Huntington collections offer information on the legal aspects of how the railroads grew and used their power.

Significant United States Supreme Court decisions pertaining to the legal status of railroad corporations and the freedom they enjoyed to carry on business involved California companies. Various collections place the legal significance of these decisions in a broader perspective.

REAL PROPERTY

Perhaps no other issue was more central to California's early history — and especially legal history — than the struggle over land. Land became a preoccupation of many during the early decades after statehood because so much tended to hinge on using it, establishing title to it, and buying, selling, or leasing it. Virtually all the major nineteenth-century California collections at the Huntington contain some references to real property. Several collections, such as the Stearns and Dalton papers, are particularly revealing.

The multiplicity of legal issues arising under the heading of real property is reflected in its numerous subdivisions. The land involved ranged from Mexican grants, to city lots, to so-called "swamp lands," and lands to induce railroad construction to homesteads. Any understanding of California's early nineteenth-century history must include the land issue and the Huntington library provides indispensable sources for that study.

TAXATION

During the nineteenth century in California numerous taxes were collected as licenses to engage in a wide range of occupations, including the practice of law. Some of the Huntington collections provide information on these and other means of taxation and governmental revenue. Other methods and instances of taxation — property, sales, and income — are also found in some of the collections, particularly those dating from the twentieth century.

TITLE

The centrality of land to California's nineteenth-century history made the settlement or quieting of titles especially important. Under this subject heading collections are noted that contain considerable material detailing litigation over title to land. Much of this litigation stemmed from the efforts to confirm Mexican grants before a specially created Board of Land Commissioners and appeals taken to California's federal district courts and the United States Supreme Court. Although the federal law reports and case files provide information on such litigation and its results, the Huntington collections provide a detailed look at the extra-judicial aspects of land litigation. The perception of the land claimants toward the process, and their strategies and efforts to bring about decisions by lobbying Congress and executive officers is amply documented.

Apart from the law suits collateral to Mexican land grant litigation that ended up in state courts, many other suits were brought to settle title to land, especially in San Francisco, Sacramento, and Los Angeles.

TORTS

The field of torts covers a wide range of civil wrongs which gave rise to causes of action for damages or relief. A number of the collections contain information on law suits dealing with such matters as defamation, libel, and wrongful death. During the latter half of the nineteenth century the expansion of railroads was accompanied by a corresponding increase in the number of accidents associated with their operation. The rise of American tort law was largely related to the growth of railroads and to some extent the Huntington collections reflect this development.

WATER

Water in California has long been a key resource in the development of the state. Water figured in the early conflicts over the diversion of rivers and use of water power to exploit the discovery of gold to the later struggles over the diversion of water to support urban populations and agriculture. A substantial number of the Huntington collections contain materials and correspondence that involve this important natural resource.

SUBJECT ACCESS GUIDE

Subject Hdgs./ Subdivision	*Collection*	*Box*	*Date*	*Finder's Aid*
ADMIRALTY				
	Fernald, Charles	4	1888	W. L. Hardison to Charles Fernald (various)
	Haight, Henry	5	1859	Card v. Steamer Goliath
	Halleck, Peachy, Billings	2(HM43003)	1851	Complaint & sworn statement of witnesses in collision case: Biley vs The Steamer
	Halleck, Peachy, Billings	2	1851	Ferand v. Hernan Cortes
	Halleck, Peachy, Billings	2	1851	Bailey v. Steamer New World
	Leidesdorff, William A.	1	1844	William Hooper to Thomas O. Larkin
	Leidesdorff, William A.	3	1847	Edward J. Dunn to Leidesdorff
	Markham, H. H.	6	1885	Charles J. Ellis to H. H. Markham
Bankruptcy	Graves, Jackson A.	10	1901	Bank of San Pedro to Henry O'Melveny
	Fernald, Charles	4	1885	Pacific Coast Steamship Co to Charles Fernald
	Catlin, Amos P.	5	1850	John Currey (atty) to Amos Catlin Sacramento)
AGRICULTURE				
Citrus Business	Azusa-Foothill	1	1902-08	Azusa-Foothill Citrus Co. Minute Book

Subject Hdgs./ Subdivision	*Collection*	*Box*	*Date*	*Finder's Aid*
AGRICULTURE (cont.)				
Citrus Business	Bacon, Henry Doug.	38-41	1860-90	Marengo Ranch Papers
Citrus Business	Graves, Jackson A.	11	1918	Jackson A. Graves to I. W. Hellman
Citrus Business	Graves, Jackson A.	8	1899	Isaias Hellman to J. A. Graves
Citrus Business	Graves, Jackson A.	2	1893	A. J. Hechtman to J. A. Graves
Citrus Business	Graves, Jackson A.	2	1894	A. J. Hechtman to J. A. Graves
Citrus Business	Graves, Jackson A.	4	1896	H. W. O'Melveny to George H. Peck
Citrus Business	Graves, Jackson A.	5	1897	Earl Fruit Co. to J. A. Graves
Citrus Business	Markham, H. H.	8	1882	Hixson, Justi & Co. to H. H. Markham (various)
Citrus Business	Shorb, James de Barth	10	1885	James Bettner to James de Barth Shorb
Citrus Business	Shorb, James de Barth	10	1886	Bettner & Chubb to James de Barth Shorb
Citrus Business	Shorb, James de Barth	79	1892	Charles W. Mott to James de Barth Shorb
Citrus Business	Shorb, James de Barth	10	1883-87	D. Biagi & Co. to James de Barth Shorb (various)
Citrus Business	Shorb, James de Barth	18	1893	Calif. Fruit Co. to James de Barth Shorb
Citrus Business	Shorb, James de Barth	28	1884-85	William T. Coleman to James de Barth Shorb (various)
Citrus Business	Shorb, James de Barth	29	1885-87	William T. Coleman & Co. to James de Barth Shorb (various)
Citrus Business	Shorb, James de Barth	30	1885-86	William T. Coleman & Co. to James M. Tiernan (various)
Citrus Business	Shorb, James de Barth	32	1891	Jeremiah Cozad to Arpad Hartaszthy and various others

Subject Hdgs./ Subdivision	Collection	Box	Date	Finder's Aid
AGRICULTURE (cont.)				
Citrus Business	Shorb, James de Barth	33	1889	A. Crihi to James de Barth Shorb
Citrus Business	Shorb, James de Barth	34	1884-90	Dalton Bros. Co. to James de Barth Shorb (various)
Citrus Business	Shorb, James de Barth	37	1885-92	John R. Dobbins to various
Citrus Business	Shorb, James de Barth	43	1884-87	Eveleth & Nash to James de Barth Shorb (various)
Citrus Business	Shorb, James de Barth	55	1883	Henderson & Sewall to James de Barth Shorb (various)
Citrus Business	Shorb, James de Barth	55	1886	Charles Hewitt to James de Barth Shorb
Citrus Business	Shorb, James de Barth	57	1885	Hixson, Justi & Co. to James de Barth Shorb (various)
Citrus Business	Shorb, James de Barth	67	1892	Richard Lee to James de Barth Shorb
Citrus Business	Shorb, James de Barth	67	1886	B. M. Lelong to James de Barth Shorb
Citrus Business	Shorb, James de Barth	71	1883-93	Lusk (A.) & Co. to various
Citrus Business	Shorb, James de Barth	98	1885	George Rice to James de Barth Shorb
Citrus Business	Shorb, James de Barth	99	1886	Erskine M. Ross to James de Barth Shorb
Citrus Business	Shorb, James de Barth	106	1886	James de Barth Shorb to George Rice
Citrus Business	Shorb, James de Barth	89	1893	Charles F. Oldham to James de Barth Shorb
Citrus Business	Shorb, James de Barth	89	1885-86	Orange Growers Protective Union of Southern California to James de Barth Shorb (various)

Subject Hdgs./ Subdivision	*Collection*	*Box*	*Date*	*Finder's Aid*
AGRICULTURE (cont.)				
Citrus Business	Shorb, James de Barth	90	1884-88	Pacific Fruit Co. to James de Barth Shorb (various)
Citrus Business	Shorb, James de Barth	92	1883-85	Peycke Bros. Co. to James de Barth Shorb (various)
Citrus Business	Shorb, James de Barth	77	1891	George Mitchell to James de Barth Shorb
Citrus Business	Shorb, James de Barth	78	1885	Ed R. Morris to James de Barth Shorb
Citrus Business	Shorb, James de Barth	80	1892	William Murray to James M. Tiernan
Citrus Business	Shorb, James de Barth	94	1883-93	Porter Brothers Co. to Various
Citrus Business	Shorb, James de Barth	101	1883-90	Scatena (L.) and Co. to James de Barth Shorb (various)
Citrus Business	Shorb, James de Barth	103	1894	Spencer K. Sewall to Maria Shorb
Citrus Business	Shorb, James de Barth	110	1887	Sleavin & Broderick to James de Barth Shorb
Citrus Business	Shorb, James de Barth	117	1883-86	W. R. Strong & Co. to Various
Citrus Business	Shorb, James de Barth	103	1894	Spencer K. Sewall to Maria Shorb
Citrus Business	Shorb, James de Barth	110	1887	Sleavin & Broderick to James de Barth Shorb
Citrus Business	Shorb, James de Barth	117	1883-86	W. R. Strong & Co. to Various
Citrus Business	Shorb, James de Barth	120	1885-86	Tiffany Refrigerator Car Co. to James de Barth Shorb (various)
Citrus Business	Shorb, James de Barth	120	1885	Transcontinental Association to James de Barth Shorb (various)

Subject Hdgs./ Subdivision	*Collection*	*Box*	*Date*	*Finder's Aid*
AGRICULTURE (cont.)				
Citrus Business	Shorb, James de Barth	121	1883-88	Truckee Lumber Co. to James de Barth Shorb (various)
Citrus Business	Shorb, James de Barth	121	1885	Union Pacific Railway Co. to Various
Citrus Business	Shorb, James de Barth	131	1868	Benjamin D. Wilson to James de Barth Shorb (various)
Citrus Business	Shorb, James de Barth	132	1868-69	Benjamin D. Wilson to Maria Shorb (various)
Citrus Business	Wolfskill, Lewis	4	1874-77	Various Centinela Orchard papers
Citrus Business	Wolfskill, Lewis	6	1877	Littlefield, Webb & Co. to Lewis Wolfskill
Citrus Business	Wolfskill, Lewis	8	1878	Various regarding Centinela Orchard
Fencing	Jacks, David	C(1)	1869	Judson Parsons to David Jacks
Fencing	Jacks, David	C(1)	1879	J. H. McDougall to David Jacks
Title	Jacks, David	BV414	1860	Jacks to Manuel Apezarena
Title	Jacks, David	BV414	1909	Jacks & Ashley to Rutherford
Title	Jacks, David	BIII8	1872	266 acres (Jacks) to D. Hargins
Title	Jacks, David	BV414	1880	Jacks to Antoneli & Manual Rodgers
Title	Jacks, David	BV414	1862	D. R. Ashley & Jacks to Jose Botellen
Title	Jacks, David	C6	1887	C. S. Gates to Jacks
Title	Jacks, David	BV414	N.D.	Jacks to Pedro Gonzales
Wine Business	Shorb, James de Barth	5	1884-81	George Arbuthnot to Various
Wine Business	Shorb, James de Barth	82	1888	Francis Newlands to James de Barth Shorb

Subject Hdgs./ Subdivision	*Collection*	*Box*	*Date*	*Finder's Aid*
AGRICULTURE (cont.)				
Wine Business	Shorb, James de Barth	82	1889	Francis Newlands to James de Barth Shorb
Wine Business	Shorb, James de Barth	84	1889	Paul Oeker to Pelham W. Ames
Wine Business	Shorb, James de Barth	84	1890	Paul Oeker to George Arbuthnot
Wine Business	Shorb, James de Barth	84	1886-87	Paul Oeker to James de Barth Shorb (various)
Wine Business	Shorb, James de Barth	85	1887	Paul Oeker to James de Barth Shorb (various)
Wine Business	Shorb, James de Barth	86	1887-88	Paul Oeker to James de Barth Shorb (various)
Wine Business	Shorb, James de Barth	87	1888	Paul Oeker to James de Barth Shorb (various)
Wine Business	Shorb, James de Barth	88	1889	Paul Oeker to James de Barth Shorb (various)
Wine Business	Shorb, James de Barth	93	1885	James M. Pitts to James de Barth Shorb
Wine Business	Shorb, James de Barth	96	1889	Purity Wine Co. of California to James de Barth Shorb (various)
Wine Business	Shorb, James de Barth	101	1890-93	San Gabriel Wine Co. to Various
Wine Business	Shorb, James de Barth	102	1887-88	Aug von Schilling to James de Barth Shorb (various)
Wine Business	Shorb, James de Barth	103	1892	Winfield Scott to James de Barth Shorb
Wine Business	Shorb, James de Barth	109	1884	Joseph C. Shorb to James de Barth Shorb
Wine Business	Shorb, James de Barth	103	1892	Winfield Scott to James de Barth Shorb
Wine Business	Shorb, James de Barth	109	1884	Joseph C. Shorb to James de Barth Shorb
Wine Business	Shorb, James de Barth	122	1888-89	U. S. Dept. of Agriculture to Various

Subject Access Guide

Subject Hdgs./ Subdivision	*Collection*	*Box*	*Date*	*Finder's Aid*
AGRICULTURE (cont.)				
Wine Business	Shorb, James de Barth	125	1885-92	Edward L. Watkins to James de Barth Shorb (various)
Wine Business	Shorb, James de Barth	127	1891	George West to James de Barth Shorb (various)
Wine Business	Shorb, James de Barth	127	1883-91	George West to James de Barth Shorb
Wine Business	Shorb, James de Barth	127	1886-93	Clarence J. Wetmore to James de Barth Shorb (various)
Wine Business	Shorb, James de Barth	128	1883-89	John M. Wheeler to James de Barth Shorb (various)
Wine Business	Shorb, James de Barth	131	1868	Benjamin D. Wilson to James de Barth Shorb (various)
Wine Business	Shorb, James de Barth	132	1865-76	Benjamin D. Wilson to Maria Shorb (various)
Wine Business	Shorb, James de Barth	133	1886	George W. Wilson to Charles Kohler
Wine Business	Shorb, James de Barth	134	1882	Frederick W. Wood to Thomas Benton Bishop (various)
Wine Business	Shorb, James de Barth	134	1883-85	Frederick W. Wood to James de Barth Shorb (various)
Wine Business	Shorb, James de Barth	135	1885-86	Frederick W. Wood to James de Barth Shorb (various)
Wine Business	Shorb, James de Barth	136	1886	Frederick W. Wood to James de Barth Shorb (various)

Subject Hdgs./ Subdivision	*Collection*	*Box*	*Date*	*Finder's Aid*
AGRICULTURE (cont.)				
Wine Business	Shorb, James de Barth	81	1887	National Viticultural Association to James de Barth Shorb
Wine Business	Shorb, James de Barth	116	1890	Charles Stern to James de Barth Shorb
Wine Business	Shorb, James de Barth	12	1876-77	John P. Boyle to James de Barth Shorb
Wine Business	Shorb, James de Barth	15	1883-88	Calif. Brd. of State Viticultural Commissioners to James de Barth Shorb (various)
Wine Business	Shorb, James de Barth	16	1889-92	Calif. Brd. of State Viticultural Commissioners to James de Barth Shorb (various)
Wine Business	Shorb, James de Barth	17	1892-93	Calif. Brd. of State Viticultural Commissioners to James de Barth Shorb (various)
Wine Business	Shorb, James de Barth	23	1889	B. F. Clayton to James de Barth Shorb
Wine Business	Shorb, James de Barth	25	1881-83	Evan James Coleman to various
Wine Business	Shorb, James de Barth	26	1883-86	Evan James Coleman to James de Barth Shorb (various)
Wine Business	Shorb, James de Barth	27	1884-93	Evan James Coleman to various
Wine Business	Shorb, James de Barth	35	1887-92	M. Denicke to James de Barth Shorb
Wine Business	Shorb, James de Barth	36	1884	James G. deTurk to James de Barth Shorb (various)
Wine Business	Shorb, James de Barth	38	1888-90	Ethelbert Dowlen to James de Barth Shorb (various)

Subject Hdgs./ Subdivision	*Collection*	*Box*	*Date*	*Finder's Aid*
AGRICULTURE (cont.)				
Wine Business	Shorb, James de Barth	38	1886	John T. Doyle to James de Barth Shorb
Wine Business	Shorb, James de Barth	39	1890	Dreyfus (B.) & Co. to James de Barth Shorb (various)
Wine Business	Shorb, James de Barth	46	1887	John M. Foy to James de Barth Shorb
Wine Business	Shorb, James de Barth	46	1885	French Consulat to Calif. Brd. of Viticultural Commissioners
Wine Business	Shorb, James de Barth	51	1890	Gundlack & Co. to James de Barth Shorb
Wine Business	Shorb, James de Barth	51	1883-88	William Gwin to James de Barth Shorb (various)
Wine Business	Shorb, James de Barth	53	1884-90	Arpad Haraszthy to James de Barth Shorb
Wine Business	Shorb, James de Barth	54	1890	Isaias W. Hellman to James de Barth Shorb
Wine Business	Shorb, James de Barth	56	1890	Marvin R. Higgins to James de Barth Shorb
Wine Business	Shorb, James de Barth	56	1884-81	Eugene W. Hilgard to Various
Wine Business	Shorb, James de Barth	59	1887-89	Charles Webb Howard to James de Barth Shorb (various)
Wine Business	Shorb, James de Barth	60	1887-88	O. Shafter Howard to Charles Webb Howard (various)
Wine Business	Shorb, James de Barth	60	1887-89	O. Shafter Howard to James de Barth Shorb (various)
Wine Business	Shorb, James de Barth	61	1887	George Husmann to James de Barth Shorb

Subject Hdgs./ Subdivision	*Collection*	*Box*	*Date*	*Finder's Aid*
AGRICULTURE (cont.)				
Wine Business	Shorb, James de Barth	62	1889	A. A. James to Pelham W. Ames
Wine Business	Shorb, James de Barth	64	1887-88	Niles Knickerbocker to James de Barth Shorb (various)
Wine Business	Shorb, James de Barth	65	1884-85	Kohler & Frohling to James de Barth Shorb
Wine Business	Shorb, James de Barth	65	1891-93	S. V. Landt to James de Barth Shorb (various)
Wine Business	Shorb, James de Barth	73	1889	Robert McPherson to James de Barth Shorb
Wine Business	Shorb, James de Barth	74	1887-89	Marschall, Spellmand & Co. to James de Barth Shorb (various)
Wine Business	Shorb, James de Barth	98	1890	William B. Risling to James de Barth Shorb
Wine Business	Shorb, James de Barth	99	1885	Erskine M. Ross to James de Barth Shorb
Wine Business	Shorb, James de Barth	100	1886-89	San Francisco Savings Union to James de Barth Shorb (various)
Wine Business	Shorb, James de Barth	75	1889	George Maxwell to James de Barth Shorb
Wine Business	Shorb, James de Barth	76	1888	Meyer, Wilson & Co. to James de Barth Shorb
BANKING				
	Adams & Co.	4	1856	Cohen Memorandum of Alvin Adams Letter
	Bacon, Henry Douglas	2	1852-53	Bacon correspondence, various
	Bacon, Henry Douglas	3	1853-55	Bacon correspondence, various
	Bacon, Henry Douglas	4	1855-57	Bacon correspondence, various
	Bacon, Henry Douglas	5	1856-57	Bacon correspondence, various

Subject Access Guide

Subject Hdgs./ Subdivision	*Collection*	*Box*	*Date*	*Finder's Aid*
BANKING (cont.)				
	Bacon, Henry Douglas	6	1857-59	Bacon correspondence, various
	Bacon, Henry Douglas	7	1859-63	Bacon correspondence, various
	Graves, Jackson A.	11	1918	Jackson A. Graves to I. W. Hellman
	Graves, Jackson A.	11	1927	Jackson A. Graves to Henry S. Pritchett
	Graves, Jackson A.	11	1909	Various to Jackson A. Graves
	Graves, Jackson A.	11	1914	Jackson A. Graves to I. W. Hellman
	Graves, Jackson A.	11	1915	Jackson A. Graves to I. W. Hellman
	Graves, Jackson A.	11	1916	Jackson A. Graves to I. W. Hellman
	Graves, Jackson A.	11	1917	Jackson A. Graves to I. W. Hellman
	Graves, Jackson A.	11	1919	Jackson A. Graves to I. W. Hellman
	Graves, Jackson A.	2	1893	J. B. Lankershim to Graves, O'Melveny & Shankland
	Graves, Jackson A.	4	1896	Haas, Baruch & Co. to J. A. Graves, H. W. O'Melveny & J. H. Shankland
Taxation	Graves, Jackson A.	3	1895	Samuel B. Mckee to H. W. O'Melveny
COMMERCIAL LAW				
	Adams & Co.	1	1853-54	Adams & Co. Letterbook, various
	Adams & Co.	2	1855	Woods to Cohen, various
	Baker, Robert	5	1882	Arturo Bandini to Robert Baker
	Baker, Robert	2	1878	Christy & Wise to R. S. Baker
	El Dorado County Arch	#II	1855-00	Merchandizing Accounts
	Leidesdorff, William A.	2	1846	Thomas O. Larkin to W. A. Leidesdorff

California Legal History Manuscripts

Subject Hdgs./ Subdivision	*Collection*	*Box*	*Date*	*Finder's Aid*
COMMERCIAL	LAW (cont.)			
	Leidesdorff, William A.	4	1847	Stephen Smith to Leidesdorff
	Leidesdorff, William A.	4	1847	Charles Maxwell to Leidesdorff
	Leidesdorff, William A.	4	1847	Rodman Price to Leidesdorff
	Leidesdorff, William A.	5	1848	David Laughlin to Leidesdorff
	Shorb, James de Barth	2	1888	Pelham W. Ames to A. W. Latham Co.
	Shorb, James de Barth	3	1888-89	Pelham W. Ames to James de Barth Shorb (re: Am. Concentrated Must Co.) (various)
	Shorb, James de Barth	135	1885	Frederick W. Wood to James de Barth Shorb (various)
	Woodworth, Selim E.	1	1856-65	Various Woodworth & Co. business papers
Bill of Exchange	Fernald, Charles	3	1878	F. A. Cline to Charles Fernald
Brandy Trade	Shorb, James de Barth	1	1889-90	Will Aitchison to James de Barth Shorb
Legal Tender	Haight, Henry	5	1864	Fletcher Haight to Henry Haight
Legal Tender	Haight, Henry	5	1867	Charles Sawyer to Henry Haight
Legal Tender	Markham, H. H.	6	1886	T. J. Fording to H. H. Markham
Legal Tender	Stearns, Abel	85	1864	Rancho Bautista account book
Legal Tender	Stearns, Abel	37	1862	Cave Johnson Couts to Abel Stearns
Legal Tender	Stearns, Abel	37	1862	Chas. Robinson Johnson to Abel Stearns
Legal Tender	Stearns, Abel	37	1862	Chas. Robinson Johnson to Abel Stearns

Subject Hdgs./ Subdivision	*Collection*	*Box*	*Date*	*Finder's Aid*
COMMERCIAL LAW (cont.)				
Legal Tender	Wilson, Benjamin Davis	09	1863	William Edwin Boardman to Benjamin D. Wilson, Benjamin Davis
Legal Tender	Wilson, Benjamin Davis	11	1865	B. D. Wilson & Thomas H. Myles to Frank Lecouvreur
Legal Tender	Wilson, Benjamin Davis	10	1864	Crane & Brigham to B. D. Wilson
Legal Tender	Wilson, Benjamin Davis	11	1867	Invoice of Theo. Wollweber, Druggist LA. payable in U.S. Gold Coin or its equivalent
Legal Tender	Wilson, Benjamin Davis	15	1871	Payable in U.S. Gold Coin
Legal Tender	Wilson, Benjamin Davis	14	1869	Perry & Woodworth to B. J. Wilson
Legal Tender	Wilson, Benjamin Davis	11	1866	Adolf Eberhart to Benj. D. Wilson
Legal Tender	Wilson, Benjamin Davis	13	1869	P. Banning to Benj. Wilson
Legal Tender	Wilson, Benjamin Davis	01	1850	Montgomery Martin to Benjamin Wilson
Legal Tender	Wilson, Benjamin Davis	02	1851	Thomas A. Hereford to Ester Sale Hereford
Promissory Note	Center, John	1	1852	Hart & Davis to John Center
Promissory Note	Center, John	1	1853-54	Issac Thorne to John Center (various amounts and dates)
Promissory Note	Center, John	2	1857	George Knox to John Center
Promissory Note	Center, John	2	1858	F. J. Thibault to John Center
Promissory Note	Center, John	3	1860	N. B. Stine to John Center
Promissory Note	Center, John	5	1864-68	Various to John Center
Promissory Note	Center, John	6	1878-80	Various to John Center
Promissory Note	Fernald, Charles	1	1862-79	Fernald (various)

Subject Hdgs./ Subdivision	Collection	Box	Date	Finder's Aid
COMMERCIAL LAW (cont.)				
Promissory Note	Fernald, Charles	3	1876	Henry Cowell to Charles Fernald (various)
Promissory Note	Fernald, Charles	4	1881	Theodore Wetzel to Charles Fernald
Promissory Note	Fernald, Charles	4	1881	R. Hichkofler to Charles Fernald
Promissory Note	Fernald, Charles	4	1886	J. B. Shaw to Charles Fernald
Promissory Note	Haight, Henry	5	1868	Hiram Gear to Henry Haight
Promissory Note	Graves, Jackson A.	11	1916	Jackson A. Graves to I. W. Hellman
Promissory Note	Graves, Jackson A.	8	1899	Frank Gibson to Henry O'Melveny
Promissory Note	Graves, Jackson A.	2	1894	John G. North to J. A. Graves
Promissory Note	Graves, Jackson A.	5	1896	J. W. Scott to A. J. Keating
Promissory Note	Graves, Jackson A.	7	1898	A. J. Harrell to J. A. Graves
Promissory Note	Keller, Matthew	1	1855	Benjamin Eaton to Keller, Matthew
Promissory Note	Keller, Matthew	1	1857	Thomas Gentry to Keller, Matthew
Promissory Note	Keller, Matthew	3	1863	Hiram McLaughlin to Keller, Matthew
Promissory Note	Keller, Matthew	3	1876	B. F. Ryder to Keller, Matthew
Promissory Note	Keller, Matthew	3	1856	Charles Taylor to Keller, Matthew
Promissory Note	Keller, Matthew	2	1872	On Commercial Promissory Note Forms
Promissory Note	Keller, Matthew	2	1856	On Commercial Promissory Note Forms
Promissory Note	Leidesdorff, Wm. A.	1	1842	Wm. Hinckley to James Watson
Promissory Note	Leidesdorff, Wm. A.	2	1846	Thomas O. Larkin to W. W. Leidesdorff
Promissory Note	Markham, H. H.	7	1890	L. T. Garnsey to H. H. Markham

Subject Access Guide

Subject Hdgs./ Subdivision	*Collection*	*Box*	*Date*	*Finder's Aid*
COMMERCIAL LAW (cont.)				
Promissory Note	Shorb, James de Barth	122	1888	Hiram A. Unruh to James de Barth Shorb
Promissory Note	Stimson, Marshall	10	1912-41	Various
Promissory Note	Wilson, Benjamin Davis	10	1864	Murray Morrison to Banjamin Davis
Promissory Note	Wolfskill, Lewis	2	1869	Adams & Wolfskill to Hayward & Company
Promissory Note	Wolfskill, Lewis	2	1872	M. R. Pleasants to Francisca Wolfskill Shepherd
Promissory Note	Wolfskill, Lewis	2	1872-78	Various of Lewis Wolfskill
Promissory Note	Wolfskill, Lewis	4	1874	Emiglio Castro & Leonardo Flores to Francisco Valenzuela
Promissory Note	Wolfskill, Lewis	5	1875	Valencia & Wolfskill to Elton
Promissory Note	Wolfskill, Lewis	5	1875	J. Fryer to Temple & Workman
Promissory Note	Wolfskill, Lewis	6	1876	Arthur Bullock to Temple & Workman
Promissory Note	Wolfskill, Lewis	6	1876	Julius Morris to Lewis Wolfskill
Promissory Note	Wolfskill, Lewis	6	1876-77	Various to Wolfskill
Promissory Note	Wolfskill, Lewis	7	1877	Lewis Wolfskill to Samuel Hellman
Promissory Note	Wolfskill, Lewis	8	1878	John Carrillo to Lewis Wolfskill (various others)
Sales	Fernald, Charles	4	1882	C. F. Bassett to Charles Fernald (various)
Sales	Jones, Elbert P.	1	1848	Record of Transfer Book
Sales	Markham, H. H.	18	1896	R. B. Taylor to H. H. Markham
Sales	Markham, H. H.	10	1884	G. W. Lechler to H. H. Markham

Subject Hdgs./ Subdivision	*Collection*	*Box*	*Date*	*Finder's Aid*
CONSTITUTIONAL LAW				
	Baker, Robert	3	1879	Edward F. Beale to Robert Baker
	Baker, Robert	3	1879	Charles Forbes to R. S. Baker (various)
	Bowron, Fletcher	33	1939	Statement...May 12, 1939
	Bowron, Fletcher	33	1942	Remarks... Police Officers Assoc. Oct. 23, 1942
	Bowron, Fletcher	42	1965-67	Harold Kennedy anti-communist various documents and opinions
	Haight, Henry	5	1861	Henry Haight to George Bissell: (Sucession of South)
	Haight, Henry	5	1868	William A. Scott to Henry Haight
	Haight, Henry	6	1871	Herschel V. Johnson to Henry Haight
	Mandeville, James Wylie	5	1854	William Stow to James Mandeville
	Mandeville, James Wylie	7	1856	John Purdy to James Mandeville
	Markham, H. H.	6	1896	T. W. Eby to H. H. Markham
	Markham, H. H.	13	1885	William Morrow to H. H. Markham
	Shorb, James de Barth	44	1884	Stephen J. Field to James de Barth Shorb
	Shorb, James de Barth	70	1886	L. A. Trades & Labor Council to James de Barth Shorb
	Shorb, James de Barth	128	1889	Stephen M. White to James de Barth Shorb
	Stanton, Philip Ackley	1	1915	L. B. Hanna to Philip Stanton

Subject Hdgs./ Subdivision	*Collection*	*Box*	*Date*	*Finder's Aid*
CONSTITUTIONAL LAW (cont.)				
Apportionment	Markham, H. H.	10	1884	Montague Leverson to H. H. Markham
Birth Control	Park, Alice Locke	3	1912	Clara S. Foltz to Alice Park
Birth Control	Park, Alice Locke	6	1925-31	Alice Park - Margaret Sanger Correspondence
Counties	Fernald, Charles	4	1883	J. T. Boyd to Charles Fernald
Sabbath	Mandeville, James Wylie	2	1853	George Patrick to Assembly
Sabbath	Mandeville, James Wylie	2	1853	C. G. Snow to James Mandeville
Sabbath	Mandeville, James Wylie	2	1853	P. L. Solomon to James Mandeville
Sabbath	Mandeville, James Wylie	3	1853	James Appleton to James Mandeville
Suffrage	Park, Alice Locke	1	1896-09	Harry Blackwell to Alice Park (various)
Suffrage	Park, Alice Locke	1	1902-09	Lydia Commander to Alice Park (various)
Suffrage	Park, Alice Locke	1	1906-07	Helen Gorgar to Alice Park (various)
Suffrage	Park, Alice Locke	1	1906-11	Ellen Sargent to Alice Park (various)
Suffrage	Park, Alice Locke	1	1907-08	Reports of California Club, Humane Education Committee, Chair, Alice Park
Suffrage	Park, Alice Locke	1	1908-10	Alice Park for Calif Equal Suffrage Assn to Mrs. MacBean
Suffrage	Park, Alice Locke	2	1909-11	Sofia Loebinger to Alice Park (various)
Suffrage	Park, Alice Locke	2	1909-11	Elizabeth Watson to Alice Park (various)

Subject Hdgs./ Subdivision	Collection	Box	Date	Finder's Aid
CONSTITUTIONAL LAW (cont.)				
Suffrage	Park, Alice Locke	2	1909-12	Mary Keith to Alice Park (various)
Suffrage	Park, Alice Locke	2	1909-12	Mary Peck to Alice Park (various)
Suffrage	Park, Alice Locke	2	1909-12	Anna Shaw to Alice Park (various)
Suffrage	Park, Alice Locke	2	1910	Florence Hartnell to Alice Park
Suffrage	Park, Alice Locke	3	1911	Alice Park to Agnes Downing
Suffrage	Park, Alice Locke	3	1911	Alice Park to Omar Garwood
Suffrage	Park, Alice Locke	3	1911	Various to Alice Park
Suffrage	Park, Alice Locke	3	1923	Clara S. Foltz to Alice Park
Suffrage	Park, Alice Locke	4	1912	Various to Alice Park
Suffrage	Park, Alice Locke	4	1912	Alice Park to various newspaper editors
Suffrage	Park, Alice Locke	4	1912	Louise Hall to Alice Park
Suffrage	Park, Alice Locke	5	1913	Various to Alice Park
Suffrage	Park, Alice Locke	5	1913	Alice Park to various
Suffrage	Park, Alice Locke	5	1915-16	Lucy Barnes to Alice Park
Suffrage	Park, Alice Locke	8	1911-20	Various entries "Park biography"
CONTRACTS				
	Adams & Co.	1	1853	Woods & Cohen & Co.
	Adams & Co.	1	1854	Cohen, etc. to purchase lumber
	Baker, Robert	1	1877	Arcadia Baker & Savage & Son
	Barclay, Henry	4	1885	Lytle Creek Water Co, & Bryon Waters (Rancho Muscupiabe)
	Bard, Thomas R.	4	1900s	Bard contracts & related papers

Subject Hdgs./ Subdivision	*Collection*	*Box*	*Date*	*Finder's Aid*
CONTRACTS (cont.)				
	Bowron, Fletcher	4	1933	Beverly Dairies, LTD. to O. T. Cook
	Center, John	2	1858	Issac Thorne to John Center
	Center, John	3	1859	Edward Bosqui to John Center
	Center, John	4	1863	F. F. Fargo to John Center
	Center, John	4	1863	Inyo Mining Co. and John Center
	Center, John	4	1863	John Center and Hugh McCormick
	Chipman-Dwinelle	2	1875	Caroline Chipman, et al disposal real estate and proceeds
	Chipman-Dwinelle	2	1863	Thomas Valentine & W. W. Chipman; Sale of San Francisco land
	Chipman-Dwinelle	1	1863	Gilbert Fancher & Placido Vega to buy guns, ship to Mexico
	Chipman-Dwinelle	2	1872	Sale of Mining Properties between J. S. Slauson & Charles Marshall
	Chipman-Dwinelle	2	1872	J. S. Slauson and J. W. Dwinelle
	Chipman-Dwinelle	2	1890	S. Stuart and C. D. Chipman Dwinelle
	Chipman-Dwinelle	2	1862-67	Various W. W. Chipman for Legal Services
	Couts, Cave J.	84	1875-30	Various Legal Papers
	Crank, James F.	2	1881-87	James Crank to various in Letterbooks
	Crank, James F.	3	1887-89	James Crank to various in Letterbooks

Subject Hdgs./ Subdivision	*Collection*	*Box*	*Date*	*Finder's Aid*
CONTRACTS (cont.)				
	Crank, James F.	3	1890-91	James Crank to various in 3 Letterbooks
	Crank, James F.	8	1892	John Sexton to A. J. Binney
	Fernald, Charles	3	1869	John Green to Charles Fernald (various)
	Fernald, Charles	6	1875	Charles Huse to Edward Pringle
	Graves, Jackson A.	7	1898	R. M. Fellows to Henry W. O'Melveny
	Graves, Jackson A.	8	1900	Sheldon Boden to H. W. O'Melveny
	Graves, Jackson A.	8	1899	Everett Ames to H. W. O'Melveny
	Graves, Jackson A.	8	1899	Warren Gregory to Graves, O'Melveny & Shankland
	Graves, Jackson A.	1	1892	Carlos Olvera to H. W. O'Melveny
	Graves, Jackson A.	2	1893	A. F. Morrison to Henry O'Melveny
	Graves, Jackson A.	2	1893	N. Ohlandt & Co. to H. W. O'Melveny
	Graves, Jackson A.	5	1897	A. M. Edelman to J. A Graves
	Graves, Jackson A.	7	1898	Carlos Olvera to Henry W. O'Melveny
	Graves, Jackson A.	7	1898	R. H. F. Variel to Henry O'Melveny
	Haight, Henry	5	1860	Henry Naglee v. Nicholas Kittle
	Houghton, Shrmn O.	1	1849	George Gliddons to S. O. Houghton
	Keller, Matthew	2	1897	Matthew Keller & L. Hafen
	Keller, Matthew	2	1865	Matthew Keller & Abel Stearns
	Keller, Matthew	3	1866	Phelps, Dodge & Co. to Matthew Keller and Abel Stearns

Subject Hdgs./ Subdivision	*Collection*	*Box*	*Date*	*Finder's Aid*
CONTRACTS (cont.)				
	Keller, Matthew	3	1909	So. Coast Land Co. & Fletcher-Salmons Investment Co.
	Keller, Matthew	3	1909	South Coast Land Co. & Edward Fletcher
	Keller, Matthew	3	1901	Southern California Ry. Co. & George Shafer & Caroline Shafer
	Leidesdorff, William A.	1	1848	Willard Buzzell & Leidesdorff
	Leidesdorff, William A.	2	1845	Willard Bussell to W. A. Leidesdorff
	Leidesdorff, William A.	3	1846	Wm. Glover & Thomas O. Larkin
	Leidesdorff, William A.	3	1846	Stephen Smith to Leidesdorff
	Leidesdorff, William A.	3	1847	John Sinclair to Leidesdorff
	Leidesdorff, William A.	3	1847	Leidesdorff & James Biddle
	Leidesdorff, William A.	3	1847	Leidesdorff & W. H. Davis
	Leidesdorff, William A.	3	1847	Thomas O. Larkin to Leidesdorff
	Leidesdorff, William A.	4	1847	James Scott and Leidesdorff
	Leidesdorff, William A.	4	1847	William & Joe Russel
	Leidesdorff, William A.	4	1847	Joe Ham et al., John Lewis
	Leidesdorff, William A.	5	1848	Theodore Cordua & Isaac Robbins
	Leidesdorff, William A.	5	1848	Henry Cooke & U. S. Army
	Mandeville, James Wylie	3	1845	Joseph Juliand to James Mandeville
	Markham, H. H.	17	1895	W. T. Spilman to H. H. Markham

Subject Hdgs./ Subdivision	*Collection*	*Box*	*Date*	*Finder's Aid*
CONTRACTS (cont.)				
	Markham, H. H.	21	1887	George D. Webster and H. H. Markham for construction of house
	McCullough, S. L. B.	1	1873-76	McCullough to various
	Potter, Charles & Isaac	1	1916-26	Cain Irrigation Co. & Pacific Power Corp (various)
	Potter, Charles & Isaac	2	19-22	Cal-Nevada Canal, Water & Power Co. (various)
	Potter, Charles & Isaac	3	1908	Hillside Water Co. & Nevada-Calif. Power Co.
	Potter, Charles & Isaac	3	1910	Hillside Water Co. to Clarence Brown
	Potter, Charles & Isaac	4	1919	Edson Adams and Arthur West
	Potter, Charles & Isaac	5	1911-24	The Sierras Construction Co. (various)
	Potter, Charles & Isaac	6	1905-30	Southern Sierra Power Co. (various)
	Potter, Charles & Isaac	7	1913	W. T. Grant & J. C. Anton & Delos A. Chappell
	Russell, Majors & Waddell	5	1861	Pony Express contract of Central Overland Calif. & Pikes Peak Express Co. and Overland Mail Co.
	Russell, Majors & Waddell	5	1861	Western State Co., Central Calif. & Pikes Peak Express Co. & Overland Mail Co.
	Shorb, James de Barth	1	1889	James Allen to James de Barth Shorb

Subject Hdgs./ Subdivision	*Collection*	*Box*	*Date*	*Finder's Aid*
CONTRACTS (cont.)				
	Shorb, James de Barth	21	1893	Chino Valley Beet Sugar Co. to James de Barth Shorb
	Shorb, James de Barth	23	1888-93	Stephen Clark to James de Barth Shorb
	Shorb, James de Barth	47	1888	William C. Furney to James de Barth Shorb
	Shorb, James de Barth	91	1891	Pasadena Stem Laundry Co. to James M. Tiernan
	Shorb, James de Barth	79	1891-92	Leroy E. Mosher to James de Barth Shorb (various)
	Shorb, James de Barth	79	1887	John Mullen to James de Barth Shorb
	Shorb, James de Barth	94	1887	Jerome Porter to James de Barth Shorb
	Shorb, James de Barth	102	1888	Aug von Schilling to Paul Oeker
	Shorb, James de Barth	121	1889	Union Construction Co. to James de Barth Shorb
	Wolfskill, Lewis	1	1862	Alexander to Dominguez of cattle and brand & ear mark rights
	Wolfskill, Lewis	1	1865	Henry Dalton to Francis Pioche to partition Rancho Azusa & San Francisquito
	Wolfskill, Lewis	2	1872	Perry Goodrich & Lewis Wolfskill
	Wolfskill, Lewis	4	1874	W. A. Dalton to Lewis Wolfskill
	Wolfskill, Lewis	6	1876	Jose Rubio to Wolfskill
Breach	Graves, Jackson A.	3	1895	J. S. Chapman to John McArthur
Chattel Mortgage	Fernald, Charles	4	1885	Thomas Bell to Charles Fernald

Subject Hdgs./ Subdivision	Collection	Box	Date	Finder's Aid
CONTRACTS (cont.)				
Chattel Mortgage	Graves, Jackson A.	10	1901	J. H. Krimminger to H. W. O'Melveny
Chattel Mortgage	Graves, Jackson A.	8	1899	Isaias Hellman to J. A. Graves
Chattel Mortgage	Graves, Jackson A.	2	1894	Isaias Hellman to J. A. Graves
Chattel Mortgage	Graves, Jackson A.	2	1894	Carlos Olvera to H. W. O'Melveny
Chattel Mortgage	Graves, Jackson A.	5	1897	Balfour, Guthrie & Co. to J. A. Graves, H. W. O'Melveny & J. H. Shankland
Chattel Mortgage	Graves, Jackson A.	7	1898	Herman Hellmand to Henry W. O'Melveny
Creditors	Fernald, Charles	3	1877	E. Fawcett to Charles Fernald
Deed	Keller, Matthew	1	1874	Enrique Avila to Matthew Keller & George Hansen in Rancho Tajauta
Deed	Leidesdorff, William A.	3	1864	Robert Ridley & Leidesdorff
Deed	Leidesdorff, William A.	4	1847	George McDougal & Rodman Price
Deed	Wolfskill, Lewis	2	1868	Henry Van Valkenberg to Lewis Wolfskill in Los Angeles
Deed	Wolfskill, Lewis	2	1868	Francois Pioche & Henry Dalton to Harding & Higgins in Rancho San Francisquito
Deed	Wolfskill, Lewis	5	1875	Bouton & Magee in Rancho San Jacinto
Deed	Wolfskill, Lewis	8	1878	Elena de Wolfskill to Lewis Wolfskill, Rancho San Jacinto Nuevo
Employment	Fernald, Charles	4	1886	Justinian Caire to Charles Fernald
Employment	Fernald, Charles	7	1887	Dixon to B. F. Thomas, Attorney to represent parties, Estate

Subject Access Guide

Subject Hdgs./ Subdivision	Collection	Box	Date	Finder's Aid
CONTRACTS (cont.)				
Lawyers	Heslop Family	1	1896-97	Services to litigate Rancho Muscupiabe title and interest
	Graves, Jackson A.	5	1897	W. M. Gardiner to Henry O'Melveny
Railroad	Shorb, James de Barth	44	1887	Frank E. Fisher to Electric Improvement Co.
Real Property	Barclay, Henry	4	1895	Savings Bank of So. Cal. & H. A. Barclay
Real Property	Keller, Matthew	3	1880	Keller & Hanson to S. C. Hahne
Real Property	O'Farrell, Jasper	1	1863	Agreement to arbitration of land dispute
	Graves, Jackson A.	2	1893	A. F. Morrison to Henry O'Melveny
Warranty	Graves, Jackson A.	8	1899	Wickliffe Matthews to Graves, O'Melveny & Shankland
Water	Graves, Jackson A.	11	1918	Jackson A. Graves to I. W. Hellman
Water	Mandeville, James Wylie	7	1856	John H. Brodt to James Mandeville
Water	Morgan, William Rollin	2	1883	Timothy Donoghue to William Morgan
Water	Morgan, William Rollin	2	1885	George W. Cox to William Morgan (various)
Water	Potter, Charles & Isaac	5	1917	Frank Baum, Edward Clark and W. E. Porter
Water	Shorb, James de Barth	49	1892	Jackson A. Graves to James de Barth Shorb
CORPORATIONS				
	Azusa-Foothill Citrus	1	1902-08	Azusa-Foothill Citrus Co. papers
	Baldwin, Anita M.	4	1907-22	L. A. Racing Association
	Baldwin, Anita M.	3	1907-22	L. A. Racing Association

Subject Hdgs./ Subdivision	Collection	Box	Date	Finder's Aid
CORPORATIONS (cont.)				
	Barclay, Henry	1	1885-92	Irvington Land & Water Co. to Minute Book
	Barclay, Henry	5	1886	East Side Water Co., L. A.
	Chipman-Dwinelle	2	1887	Sierra Nevada Silver Mining Co. By-Laws
	Crank, James F.	3	1887-91	James Crank to various in 3 Letterbooks
	Crank, James F.	10	1889	Crank Memorandum on Sierra Madre
	Crank, James F.	10	1886-93	Misc. Legal papers of Sierra Madre Vintage Co.
	Crank, James F.	11	1888-93	Business Papers of L. A. Cable Ry. Co. & Pacific Ry. Co.
	Graves, Jackson A.	11	1918	Jackson A. Graves to I. W. Hellman
	Graves, Jackson A.	9	1910	A. B. McCutchen to H. W. O'Melveny
	Graves, Jackson A.	9	1900	Horace G. Platt to H. W. O'Melveny (various discussing case law)
	Graves, Jackson A.	11	1917	Jackson A. Graves to I. W. Hellman
	Graves, Jackson A.	11	1917	Hellman (Alamitos Land Co. Lease)
	Graves, Jackson A.	11	1919	Jackson A. Graves to I. W. Hellman
	Graves, Jackson A.	1	1892	Henry Malter to Graves, O'Melveny & Shankland
	Graves, Jackson A.	3	1895	Isaias Hellman to J. A. Graves
	Graves, Jackson A.	7	1898	Horace G. Platt to Henry O'Melveny
	Haight, Henry	6	1871	Henry Haight to L. T. Carr
	Keller, Matthew	1	1864-65	Arizona Consol. Mining Co. to Matthew Keller
	Markham, H. H.	4	1896	John S. Chapman to H. H. Markham

Subject Hdgs./ Subdivision	Collection	Box	Date	Finder's Aid
CORPORATIONS (cont.)				
	Morgan, William Rollin	2	1887	W. S. Chapman to William Morgan
	Potter, Charles & Isaac	2	1819-23	Cal-Nevada Canal, Water & Power Co. (various)
	Potter, Charles & Isaac	2	1917	Central Calif. Electric Co, v. Pacific Power Co. (various)
	Potter, Charles & Isaac	2	1915	Central Calif. Electric Corp. (various)
	Potter, Charles & Isaac	2	1916-28	Deseret Water, Oil & Mining Co. (various)
	Potter, Charles & Isaac	2	1918-25	Goleta Consolidated Mining Co. (various)
	Potter, Charles & Isaac	3	1916-34	Hillside Water Co. (various)
	Potter, Charles & Isaac	3	1918	Hydro-Electric Co.
	Potter, Charles & Isaac	3	1918-23	Mono County Irrigation Corp. (various)
	Potter, Charles & Isaac	4	1919-27	Mono Power Company (various)
	Potter, Charles & Isaac	4	1918	Nevada-Calif. Power Co. (various)
	Potter, Charles & Isaac	5	1922-34	Nevada-Calif. Electric Co. (various)
	Potter, Charles & Isaac	5	1910-24	Pacific Power Co. (various)
	Potter, Charles & Isaac	5	1911-29	The Sierras Construction Co. (various)
	Potter, Charles & Isaac	6	1918	The Southern Sierras Power Co. (various)

Subject Hdgs./ Subdivision	*Collection*	*Box*	*Date*	*Finder's Aid*
CORPORATIONS (cont.)				
	Potter, Charles & Isaac	6	1915-28	Southern Sierra Power Co. (various)
	Potter, Charles & Isaac	1	1915	Cain Irrigation Co. (Mono County)
	Shorb, James de Barth	2	1888	Pelham W. Ames to A. W. Latham Co.
	Shorb, James de Barth	3	1888-89	Pelham W. Ames to James de Barth Shorb (re: Am. Concentrated Must Co.) (various)
	Shorb, James de Barth	25	1882	Evan James Coleman to James de Barth Shorb (various)
	Shorb, James de Barth	26	1883-86	Evan James Coleman to James de Barth Shorb (various)
	Shorb, James de Barth	115	1884	Albert M. Stephens to James de Barth Shorb
	Shorb, James de Barth	111	1892	George H. Smith to James de Barth Shorb
	Shorb, James de Barth	111	1892	George H. Smith to James de Barth Shorb
	Wolfskill, Lewis	7	1877	William Hughes to Lewis Wolfskill
Bonds	Graves, Jackson A.	9	1900	Horace G. Platt to Henry O'Melveny
Bonds	Graves, Jackson A.	9	1900	San Gabriel Electric Co to H. W. O'Melveny
Mortgage	Shorb, James de Barth	123	1893	Robert Variel to James de Barth Shorb

Subject Hdgs./ Subdivision	*Collection*	*Box*	*Date*	*Finder's Aid*
CORPORATIONS (cont.)				
Partnership	Fernald, Charles	6	1857	Hones vs. Thompson Litigation Papers
Partnership	Keller, Matthew	2	1876	Keller, Matthew & Thomas Mahoney
Partnership	Shorb, James de Barth	38	1869	John T. Doyle to James de Barth Shorb
Partnership	Shorb, James de Barth	67	1893	George W. Lawrence to James de Barth Shorb
Taxation	Graves, Jackson A.	11	1918	Jackson A. Graves to I. W. Hellman
CRIMES				
	Aram, Joseph	1	1895	Joseph Aram to Eugene Aram
	Baldwin, Anita M.	7	1905-10	Arcadia Criminal Justice Docket
	Bowron, Fletcher	3	1948	Bowron to Charles W. Fricke
	Bowron, Fletcher	3	1948	Bowron to City Council (various)
	Bowron, Fletcher	3	1950	Bowron to John W. Snyder
	Bowron, Fletcher	42	1959	Crime Comic Book Ordinance, Harold W. Kennedy, Co. Counsel
	Bowron, Fletcher	4	1932-34	Bowron to various, misc.
	Brent, Joseph	1	1861	Calhoun Benham, William Gwin (various)
	Brent, Joseph	2	1865	Shore, John W. to Joseph L. Brent
	Brent, Joseph	2	1865	Wilson, Benjamin D. to Joseph L. Brent, July 10, 1865
	Brent, Joseph	2	1865	Banning, Phineas to Joseph L. Brent (Los Angeles)

Subject Hdgs./ Subdivision	Collection	Box	Date	Finder's Aid
CRIMES (cont.)				
	Brent, Joseph	5	1850-60	Joseph L. Brent "Life in California" (various ref.)
	Brent, Joseph	5	1852	Lugo Case
	Dane Family	1	1856-57	Lawyer's Diary, Sacramento to S.F.
	Fernald, Charles	3	1853	Charles Huse to Fernald Arroyo Buros shooting
	Ford, John Anson	29-31	1934	
	Graves, Jackson A.	1	1892	Samuel Purdy to Graves, O'Melveny & Shankland
	Haight, Henry	1	1851	Henry Haight to Samuel Haight
	Hoadley, Milo	2	1851	Hoadley's Journal 1850-52 contains observations on S.F. Vigilance movement of 1851
	Kincade, John T.	2	1856	John Kincade to James Kincade comments on 1856 S.F. Vigilance movement
	Leidesdorff, Wm. A.	1	1845	Thomas O. Larkin to J. A. Sutter
	Mandeville, James Wylie	7	1856	William Norman to James Mandeville: comments on Vigilance Committee of 1856 to San Francisco
	Mandeville, James Wylie	8	1857	P. L. Solomon to James Mandeville (various)
	Park, Alice Locke	4	1912-13	Henry S. Salt to Alice Park
	Park, Alice Locke	5	1914	Alice Park to W. P. Hunt

Subject Hdgs./ Subdivision	*Collection*	*Box*	*Date*	*Finder's Aid*
CRIMES (cont.)				
	SF Committee of Vigilance	2	1856	Investigation Committee Documents
	SF Committee of Vigilance Unclass		1853-56	S.F. Criminal Court Records
	SF Committee of Vigilance Unclass		1856	Murder of James King of William
	SF Committee of Vigilance Unclass		1856	Murder of George Kittering
	SF Committee of Vigilance Unclass		1856	David Terry's Assault on Hopkins
	Terry, David Smith	1	1852	David Terry to Cornelia Terry
	Terry, David Smith	1	1856	C. D. Tucker to Cornelia Terry
	Terry, David Smith	1	1856	David Terry to Cornelia Terry re: San Francisco Vigilance Committee
	Watkins, Louise Ward	2	1913	Louise Watkins to parents
	Watkins, Louise Ward	7	1947	Louise Watkins to Mother
Assault	Adams & Co HScrapbk	V4, p 31	1854	San Francisco Daily Herald
Assault	Jacks, David	C(7)	1889	J. B. Warren (Hollister) to David Jacks
Battery	Graves, Jackson A.	10	1901	A. A. Moore to Henry W. O'Melveny
Burglary	Adams & Co HScrap	V3, p 144	1854	San Francisco Herald
Burglary	Jacks, David	C(2)	1878	Laurence to Jacks
Contract	Jacks, David	C(8)	1890	L. H. Garrigns to David Jacks
Gambling	Woolwine, Thomas Lee	4	1916	Various to Woolwine
Grand Jury	Bowron, Fletcher	4	1934	Walter N. Mac-Adam to Bowron
Grand Jury	Bowron, Fletcher	4	1934	Bowron's instructions to 1934 L.A. County Grand Jury

Subject Hdgs./ Subdivision	*Collection*	*Box*	*Date*	*Finder's Aid*
CRIMES (cont.)				
Grand Jury	Bowron, Fletcher	42	1960	Cal. Grand Jury by Harold W. Kennedy and James W. Briggs
Homicide	Adams & Co HScrap	V4, p 73	1854	San Francisco Herald, December 23, 1854
Horse Theft	Adams & Co HScrap	V3, p 107	1854	San Francisco Daily Herald
Horse Theft	Jacks, David	C(8)	1890	David Jacks to Sheriff's Office
Liquor	Woolwine, Thomas Lee	1	1916	Woolwine to W. S. Tower
Liquor	Woolwine, Thomas Lee	1	1916	Woolwine to M. J. Garstang
Parole	Bowron, Fletcher	4	1934	H. H. Ashley to Judge Bowron
Parole	Bowron, Fletcher	4	1934	Hinton G. Clabaugh on Parole Laws
Petty Theft	Jacks, David	C(3)	1879	John Whitworth to David Jacks
Prevention	Jacks, David	C(7)	1889	Francis H. Robinson to David Jacks
Prostitution	Morgan, William Rollin	2	1879	D. H. R. to William Morgan
Prostitution	Woolwine, Thomas Lee	1	1916	Robert Barton to Woolwine
Rape	Adams & Co HScrap	V5, p 150	1855	San Francisco Daily Herald November 8, 1855
Rape	Adams & Co HScrap	V2, p 26	1853	Los Angeles Star, Sept. 20, 1853
Sanity	Bowron, Fletcher	6	1954	Bowron to Ervis W. Lester
	Haight, Henry H.	1	1851	Haight to Samuel Haight
DEBTOR AND CREDITOR				
	Graves, Jackson A.	1	1893	Richard Gird to Graves, O'Melveny & Shankland
	Adams & Co.	1	1854	Agreement to appoint receiver
	Adams & Co.	1	1854	Thompson & Co v. Ca. Lumber Mfg.

Subject Hdgs./ Subdivision	*Collection*	*Box*	*Date*	*Finder's Aid*
DEBTOR AND CREDITOR (cont.)				
	Adams & Co.	1	1855	Guarantee of Loan to Ca. Steam Navigation Co.
	Adams & Co.	2	1855	Lewis Gerstle to Alfred Cohen
	Adams & Co.	2	1855	John S. Scott to Alfred Cohen
	Adams & Co.	2	1855	Janes, Doyle, Barber & Boyd and Hackett & Casserly to Alvin Adams
	Adams & Co.	2	1855	Alfred Cohen to Alvin Adams
	Adams & Co.	2	1855	Writs of Attachment against Adams & Company
	Adams & Co.	2	1855	Charles Macy to Alfred Cohen
	Adams & Co.	2	1855	William Gough to Richard Roman, Alfred Cohen, & Edward Jones
	Adams & Co.	3	1855	Daniel Haskell to Alfred Cohen
	Adams & Co.	3	1855	E. W. Tracy to Levi Robie
	Adams & Co.	3	1855	Alfred Cohen to Hackett & Casserly
	Adams & Co.	3	1855	Gabriel Swezy to Alfred Cohen
	Adams & Co.	3	1855	Robertson, Sanderson & Hune to Alfred Cohen
	Adams & Co.	3	1855-58	Litigation papers against Alvin Adams, Adams & Co.
	Adams & Co.	4	1859	Alfred Cohen to Wallace and Rayle
	Adams & Co.	4	1861-63	Marye v. Roman case
	Bacon, Henry D.	5-21	1856-06	Bacon correspondence, various

Subject Hdgs./ Subdivision	Collection	Box	Date	Finder's Aid
DEBTOR AND CREDITOR (cont.)				
	Baker, Robert	2	1878	Crass & Co. to Robert Baker
	Baker, Robert	3	1879	Charles Forbes to Robert Baker
	Baker, Robert	3	1879	Farmers & Merchants Bank to Robert Baker
	Baldwin, Anita M.	5	1898	Wilson & Bulla to H. A. Unruh
	Center, John	1	1856	Benjamin B. Harrison to John Center
	Crank, James F.	5	1895	Blauvelt & Anderson to E. R. Hibbard
	Crank, James F.	5	1896	P. A. Demens to State Loan & Trust Co.
	Graves, Jackson A.	1	1893	Curtis, Oster, & Curtis to Graves, O'Melveny & Shankland
	Graves, Jackson A.	1	1893	Farmer & Farmer to Graves, O'Melveny & Shankland
	Graves, Jackson A.	1	1893	James M. Gully to J. A. Graves (various)
	Graves, Jackson A.	1	1893	Isaias W. Hellman to J. A. Graves
	Graves, Jackson A.	2	1893	F. B. Lane to Graves, O'Melveny & Shankland
	Graves, Jackson A.	2	1893	J. B. Lanjershim to Graves, O'Melveny & Shankland
	Graves, Jackson A.	3	1895	Edwin Booth
	Graves, Jackson A.	8	1899	A. R. Verilyea to H. W. O'Melveny
	Graves, Jackson A.	3	1895	Frank Gibson to J. A. Graves
	Graves, Jackson A.	2	1894	C. B. Grove to H. W. O'Melveny

Subject Hdgs./ Subdivision	Collection	Box	Date	Finder's Aid
DEBTOR AND CREDITOR (cont.)				
	Graves, Jackson A.	2	1894	Reinstein & Eisner to J. A. Graves, H. W. O'Melveny & J. H. Shankland
	Graves, Jackson A.	3	1894	H. E. Small to J. M. Griffith
	Graves, Jackson A.	2	1894	J. A. Graves, H. W. O'Melveny & J. H. Shankland to Sam Frankel
	Graves, Jackson A.	5	1897	A. G. Beyer to J. A. Graves (various)
	Graves, Jackson A.	11	1918	Jackson A. Graves to I. W. Hellman
	Graves, Jackson A.	11	1918	Jackson A. Graves to I. W. Hellman
	Graves, Jackson A.	11	1918	Jackson A. Graves to E. S. Heller
	Graves, Jackson A.	8	1899	W. J. Sloane Co to Graves, O'Melveny & Shankland
	Graves, Jackson A.	8	1899	Z. B. West to J. A. Graves
	Graves, Jackson A.	8	1899	Bicknell, Gibson & Trask to Henry W. O'Melveny
	Haight, Henry	5	1868	R. H. Lloyd to Henry Haight
	Haight, Henry	6	1870	William Waldo to Henry Haight
	Haight, Henry	2	1854	A. M. Gardner to Wells & Haight
	Haight, Henry	1	1851	Henry Haight to Dugald C. Haight
	Haight, Henry	1	1851	William Root to Henry Haight
	Haight, Henry	2	1853	A. M. Gardner to Wells & Haight
	Haight, Henry	2	1853	Samuel W. Haight to Samuel S. Haight
	Haight, Henry	2	1854	N. McKimmey to Wells, Haight and Gary

Subject Hdgs./ Subdivision	*Collection*	*Box*	*Date*	*Finder's Aid*
DEBTOR AND CREDITOR (cont.)				
	Haight, Henry	2	1854	Manuel Alvarez to Wells, Haight and Gary
	Haight, Henry	2	1854	George W. Lynch to Joseph Wells
	Haight, Henry	2	1854	William Wallace to Wells, Haight and Gary
	Haight, Henry	2	1854	Woods, Christy & Co. to Wells and Haight
	Haight, Henry	2	1854	Bernard Pratte to Joseph Wells
	Haight, Henry	2	1854	Samuel Treat to Joseph Wells
	Haight, Henry	3	1854	Morgan, McClung & Co. to Joseph Wells
	Haight, Henry	3	1854	Siter, Price & Co. to Wells & Haight
	Haight, Henry	3	1854	White, J. M. Underhill to Joseph Wells
	Haight, Henry	3	1854	William L. Smith to Joseph Wells
	Haight, Henry	3	1854	Acher Bates to Wells, Haight & Gary
	Haight, Henry	3	1855	William Cornwell to Haight & Gary
	Haight, Henry	3	1855	Joseph Wells to Henry Haight
	Haight, Henry	3	1856	Samuel Way to Henry Haight
	Haight, Henry	4	1856	H. Pearsons to Henry Haight
	Haight, Henry	4	1856	Joseph Wells to Henry Haight (various)
	Haight, Henry	4	1856	J. N. & C. F. Burns to Fletcher Haight
	Haight, Henry	4	1856	Samuel Way to F. M. & H. H. Haight
	Haight, Henry	4	1856	J. O. Goodwin to Henry Haight

Subject Hdgs./ Subdivision	*Collection*	*Box*	*Date*	*Finder's Aid*
DEBTOR AND CREDITOR (cont.)				
	Haight, Henry	4	1856	Joseph Brown to F. M. & H. H. Haight (various)
	Haight, Henry	4	1854	Joseph Wells to Henry Haight
	Halleck, Peachy, Billings	2	1859	Sparks v. de la Guerra
	Halleck, Peachy, Billings	2	1852	Sparks v. Kohler
	Mandeville, James Wylie	2	1853	Albert Grant to James Mandeville
	Mandeville, James Wylie	4	1854	E. W. Councilman to James Mandeville
	Mandeville, James Wylie	6	1855	Luther B. Curtiss to James Mandeville
	Markham, H. H.	13	1882	W. F. P. Noble to H. H. Markham
	Morgan, William Rollin	1	1870	W. F. Hill to William Morgan
	Morgan, William Rollin	1	1874	Henry Turner to William Morgan
	Morgan, William Rollin	2	1880	L. L. Brown to William Morgan
	Morgan, William Rollin	2	1883	Timothy Donoghue to William Morgan
	New Almaden Mine	1	1854-55	John B. Gray & Robert Walker contracts
	Russell, Majors & Waddell	4	1860	R. W. Durham to William B. Waddell
	Shorb, James de Barth	1	1888	James M. Allen to James de Barth Shorb
	Shorb, James de Barth	20	1893	Stanton L. Carter to James de Barth Shorb
	Shorb, James de Barth	69	1884	L. A. Board of Trade to James de Barth Shorb
	Shorb, James de Barth	92	1890	Cornelius Pendleton to Maria Shorb
	Shorb, James de Barth	9	1883	Alexander D. Bell to Charles Krug
	Shorb, James de Barth	12	1890	Brenda Prague Bodfish to James de Barth Shorb

Subject Hdgs./ Subdivision	Collection	Box	Date	Finder's Aid
DEBTOR AND CREDITOR (cont.)				
	Shorb, James de Barth	48	1891	Mrs. Thomas Gillett to James de Barth Shorb
	Shorb, James de Barth	48	1877	Glassell, Chapman & Smith to Isaias W. Hellman (Los Angeles Tobacco Assn.)
	Shorb, James de Barth	50	1892-93	N. Green to James de Barth Shorb
	Shorb, James de Barth	72	1885	Joseph W. McClung to James de Barth Shorb
	Shorb, James de Barth	97	1891	Peyton Randolph to James de Barth Shorb
	Shorb, James de Barth	98	1883	George Rice to James de Barth Shorb
	Shorb, James de Barth	90	1891	Charles T. Palmer to various
	Shorb, James de Barth	80	1891	William Murray to James M. Tiernan
	Shorb, James de Barth	102	1889-94	Thomas L. Schuyler to James de Barth Shorb (various)
	Shorb, James de Barth	103	1890	W. E. Scott to James dc Barth Shorb
	Shorb, James de Barth	104	1887	Frank Shay to James de Barth Shorb
	Shorb, James de Barth	109	1869	Maria Shorb to Benjamin D. Wilson
	Shorb, James de Barth	103	1890	W. E. Scott to James de Barth Shorb
	Shorb, James de Barth	104	1887	Frank Shay to James de Barth Shorb
	Shorb, James de Barth	109	1869	Maria Shorb to Benjamin D. Wilson

Subject Hdgs./ Subdivision	*Collection*	*Box*	*Date*	*Finder's Aid*
DEBTOR AND CREDITOR (cont.)				
	Shorb, James de Barth	119	1890	Crittenden Thornton to James de Barth Shorb
	Shorb, James de Barth	120	1893	Gustav Tietze to James M. Tiernan
	Shorb, James de Barth	126	1892	Joshua B. Webster to James de Barth Shorb (various)
	Shorb, James de Barth	126	1886-92	Wells, Fargo & Co. to Various
	Shorb, James de Barth	130	1892	Frank E. Williams to James M. Tiernan (various)
	Shorb, James de Barth	132	1876	Benjamin D. Wilson to Maria Shorb (various)
	Shorb, James de Barth	135	1885	Frederick W. Wood to James de Barth Shorb
	Shorb, James de Barth	136	1886	Frederick W. Wood to James de Barth Shorb (various)
	Terry, David Smith	1	1867	Dennis Oullaham to Cornelia Terry
	Watkins, Louise Ward	5	1939	Louise Watkins to Kathleen
	Wolfskill, Lewis	6	1876	Notice of Attachment
	Wolfskill, Lewis	7	1877	Honore Ramboz to Lewis Wolfskill
Admiralty	Graves, Jackson A.	10	1901	Bank of San Pedro to Henry O'Melveny
Attachment	Fernald, Charles	2	1877	Levi Taylor to Thomas Bard
Attachment	Fernald, Charles	3	1877	William W. Curtis to Charles Fernald (various)
Attachment	Fernald, Charles	6	1876	Bond for Release of Attachment, Fernald, Richards vs. Fenlon
Attachment	Graves, Jackson A.	3	1895	W. B. Johnson to Graves, O'Melveny & J. H. Shankland

Subject Hdgs./ Subdivision	Collection	Box	Date	Finder's Aid
DEBTOR AND CREDITOR (cont.)				
Attachment	Markham, H. H.	8	1897	Arthur E. Hepburn to H. H. Markham
Bankruptcy	Cameron, E. Thomas	1	1886	William McKee to Thom
Bankruptcy	Crank, James F.	4	1891-93	James Crank to various in Letterbooks
Bankruptcy	Crank, James F.	5	1891	James Hough-teling to James Crank (various)
Bankruptcy	Crank, James F.	6	1891	Joseph H. Haldley to James Crank
Bankruptcy	Crank, James F.	7	1891-92	John Mitchell to James Crank (various)
Bankruptcy	Crank, James F.	8	1892-93	Edwin B. Smith to James Crank (various)
Bankruptcy	Graves, Jackson A.	10	1901	San Gabriel Wine Co to Moreton Haig, Garvey Water Co.
Bankruptcy	Graves, Jackson A.	1	1892	Isaias W. Hellman to Jackson Graves
Bankruptcy	Graves, Jackson A.	2	1893	Victor Montgom-ery to Graves, O'Melveny & Shankland
Bankruptcy	Graves, Jackson A.	3	1894	T. C. Spelling to Rev F. Mora
Bankruptcy	Graves, Jackson A.	5	1897	L. W. Blinn Lum-ber Co. to So. Cal. Power Co.
Bankruptcy	Graves, Jackson A.	5	1897	L. W. Blinn Lumber Co. to H. W. O'Melveny
Bankruptcy	Haight, Henry	4	1857	Robert Haight to Samuel Haight

Subject Hdgs./ Subdivision	*Collection*	*Box*	*Date*	*Finder's Aid*
DEBTOR AND CREDITOR (cont.)				
Bankruptcy	New Almaden Mine		1860	To "Dear Judge"
Bankruptcy	Shorb, James de Barth	45	1884	Albert E. Fletcher to James de Barth Shorb
Bankruptcy	Shorb, James de Barth	63	1893	William G. Kerckhoff to James de Barth Shorb
Deed	Graves, Jackson A.	88-89 LB	1888	Graves, O'Melveny & Shankland to Asa Ellis
Garnishment	Fernald, Charles	3	1876	Charles Cobb to Charles Fernald
Garnishment	Graves, Jackson A.	4	1896	Chico Valley Beet Sugar Co. to H. W. O'Melveny
Mechanic's Lien	Baker, Robert	1	1878	Lawrence Gottig to Jerome Lincoln
Mechanic's Lien	Baker, Robert	1	1878	Lovell White to Jerome Lincoln
Mechanic's Lien	Graves, Jackson A.	5	1896	Robert Smilie to J. A. Graves, H. W. O'Melveny & J. H. Shankland
Mechanic's Lien	Graves, Jackson A.	4	1896	L. W. Blinn Lumber Co., to J. A. Graves, H. W. O'Melveny & J. H. Shankland
Mechanic's Lien	Markham, H. H.	19	1890	Wilson & Bulla to H. H. Markham
Mechanic's Lien	Graves, Jackson A.	4	1895	San Pedro Lumber to J. A. Graves, H. W. O'Melveny & J. H. Shankland
ENVIRONMENTAL LAW				
	Bowron, Fletcher	33	1939	Address: L. A. Co. Conservation Congress
	Ford, John Anson	22-23	1943	1858 L. A. Air Pollution papers
	Shorb, James de Barth	11	1887	Thomas Benton Bishop to August Mayer
Air Pollution	Bowron, Fletcher	3	1950	Bowron to A. I. Stewart

Subject Hdgs./ Subdivision	*Collection*	*Box*	*Date*	*Finder's Aid*
ENVIRONMENTAL LAW (cont.)				
Air Pollution	Bowron, Fletcher	2	1946	Albine P. Norton to J. Allen Chapman
Air Pollution	Bowron, Fletcher	3	1948	Bowron to June Thompson
ESTATES				
	Baldwin, Anita M.	1	1913	Estate Papers, Elias Baldwin
	Baldwin, Anita M.	6	1929-31	Estate Papers, Clara Stocker
	Baldwin, Anita M.	6	88-18	Estate Papers, Elias Jackson
	Baldwin, Anita M.	5	1912	Estate Papers, Elias Baldwin
	Center, John	5	1884	Frances Fleming Estate documents
	Chipman-Dwinelle	2	1916-39	Josephine Phelps Will Litigation Papers
	Chipman-Dwinelle	1	1923	William Chipman to Fannie Chipman
	Chipman-Dwinelle	2	1862-64	Horace Jones Estate Papers
	Couts, Cave Johnson	74	1914-35	Arcadia (Bandini) Stearns Baker Estate Papers
	Couts, Cave Johnson	74	1894-96	Jeremiah W. Clemens Estate Papers
	Couts, Cave Johnson	74	1865-26	Cave Couts Estate papers
	Couts, Cave Johnson	83	1887-08	Cave Couts Estate Papers
	Couts, Cave Johnson	84	1898-08	Isidora (Bandini) Couts Estate Papers
	Fernald, Charles	3	1872	Adam R. Magraw to Fernald & Richards (various)
	Fernald, Charles	3	1876	H. S. Dixon to Charles Fernald (various)
	Fernald, Charles	3	1876	J. D. Hines to Charles Fernald (various)
	Fernald, Charles	3	1877	J. S. Alemany to Charles Fernald (various)

Subject Hdgs./ Subdivision	*Collection*	*Box*	*Date*	*Finder's Aid*
ESTATES (cont.)				
	Fernald, Charles	3	1877	W. J. Graves to Charles Fernald (various-Hartnell estate)
	Fernald, Charles	3	1877	John H. Platt to Charles Fernald
	Fernald, Charles	3	1877	R. C. Rogers to Charles Fernald
	Fernald, Charles	3	1878	A. J. Jeghers to Charles Fernald (various)
	Fernald, Charles	3	1878	Pringle & Hayne to Charles Fernald (various)
	Fernald, Charles	4	1881	John W. Ryland to Charles Fernald
	Fernald, Charles	4	1882	Bion Bradbury to Charles Fernald
	Fernald, Charles	4	1881	Theodore Wetzel to Charles Fernald
	Fernald, Charles	4	1885	Thomas Bell to Charles Fernald
	Fernald, Charles	4	1885	L. C. McKeeby to Charles Fernald
	Fernald, Charles	4	1885	Wilson and Wilson to Charles Fernald (various)
	Fernald, Charles	4	1886	Henry Newhall to Charles Fernald
	Fernald, Charles	4	1886	L. C. McKeeby to Charles Fernald
	Fernald, Charles	4	1889	Charles Fernald to Henry Newhall
	Fernald, Charles	4	1890	A. Webb to Charles Fernald
	Fernald, Charles	5	1871	Fernald & Richards to A. R. Magraw
	Fernald, Charles	5	1876	Charles Fernald to Charles Huse
	Fernald, Charles	6	1865	Probate file Scott vs. Chapman
	Fernald, Charles	6	1871	Probate file Reed vs. Huse

Subject Hdgs./ Subdivision	*Collection*	*Box*	*Date*	*Finder's Aid*
ESTATES (cont.)				
	Fernald, Charles	6	1878	Probate file Huse, Hill vs. Den
	Fernald, Charles	6	1889	Probate file Estate of Packard
	Fernald, Charles	6	1890	Probate file Estate of Merced Cota de Solari
	Fernald, Charles	7	1871-73	Probate file Estate of Henry S. Morgan, San Francisco Probate Court
	Fernald, Charles	7	1864	Estate papers, E. B. Williams
	Graves, Jackson A.	11	1920	Jackson A. Graves to E. S. Heller
	Graves, Jackson A.	9	1900	L. N. Franl to H. W. O'Melveny
	Graves, Jackson A.	9	1900	Mississippi Valley Trust Co. to Henry W. O'Melveny
	Graves, Jackson A.	10	1901	Title Insurance & Trust Co to Graves, O'Melveny & Shankland
	Graves, Jackson A.	11	1914	Jackson A. Graves to I. W. Hellman
	Graves, Jackson A.	11	1919	Jackson A. Graves to I. W. Hellman
	Graves, Jackson A.	10	1901	Luis Arques to H. W. O'Melveny
	Graves, Jackson A.	10	1901	F. A. Hihn to J. H. Graves
	Graves, Jackson A.	10	1901	A. A. Moore to H. W. O'Melveny
	Graves, Jackson A.	8	1899	L. N. Frank to J. A. Graves, O'Melveny & Shankland
	Graves, Jackson A.	8	1899	Title Insurance & Trust Co to Garve, O'Melveny & Shankland
	Graves, Jackson A.	8	1899	John D. Works to Henry O'Melveny
	Graves, Jackson A.	8	1900	Luis Arques to H. W. O'Melveny

Subject Hdgs./ Subdivision	*Collection*	*Box*	*Date*	*Finder's Aid*
ESTATES (cont.)				
	Graves, Jackson A.	8	1900	Carter, Hughes, & Dwight to Graves, O'Melveny and Shankland
	Graves, Jackson A.	8	1899	E. J. LeBreton to J. A. Graves
	Graves, Jackson A.	8	1899	Gutsch & Leowy to Graves, O'Melveny & Shankland
	Graves, Jackson A.	1	1893	John D. Bicknell to J. A. Graves
	Graves, Jackson A.	1	1893	Isaias W. Hellman to J. A. Graves
	Graves, Jackson A.	2	1893	Carlos Olvera to H. W. O'Melveny
	Graves, Jackson A.	2	1893	Wells, Monroe & Lee to William R. Howland
	Graves, Jackson A.	3	1895	Allen & Flint to H. W. O'Melveny
	Graves, Jackson A.	3	1895	Luis Arques to H. W. O'Melveny (various)
	Graves, Jackson A.	3	1895	R. B. Berry to Graves, O'Melveny & Shankland
	Graves, Jackson A.	3	1895	F. B. Daly to J. A. Graves, H. W. O'Melveny & J. H. Shankland
	Graves, Jackson A.	2	1894	R. B. Berrey to various
	Graves, Jackson A.	2	1894	Isaias Hellman to J. A. Graves

Subject Hdgs./ Subdivision	*Collection*	*Box*	*Date*	*Finder's Aid*
ESTATES (cont.)				
	Graves, Jackson A.	2	1894	Loewy & Gutsh to J. A. Graves, H. W. O'Melveny & J. H. Shankland
	Graves, Jackson A.	4	1896	Isaias W. Hellman to J. A. Graves
	Graves, Jackson A.	4	1896	Joseph Rothschild to James H. Shankland
	Graves, Jackson A.	3	1895	Loewy & Gutsch to Graves, O, M & Sh
	Graves, Jackson A.	4	1895	Maurice S. Hellman to J. A. Graves, H. W. O'Melveny & J. H. Shankland
	Graves, Jackson A.	4	1895	Charles M. Stephens to I. W. Hellman
	Graves, Jackson A.	4	1896	A. A. Moore, Jr. to J. A. Graves
	Graves, Jackson A.	4	1896	Luis Arques to H. W. O'Melveny
	Graves, Jackson A.	5	1897	Luis Arques to H. W. O'Melveny
	Graves, Jackson A.	7	1898	Works, Works, and Ingle to Henry O'Melveny
	Graves, Jackson A.	5	1897	Ralph Follows to Henry O'Melveny
	Graves, Jackson A.	6	1897	Carlos Olvera to H. W. O'Melveny
	Graves, Jackson A.	7	1898	Frank Gibson to J. A. Graves, H. W. O'Melveny & J. H. Shankland
	Graves, Jackson A.	7	1898	French Savings Bank to J. Graves, E. J. L. Breton for Bank
	Graves, Jackson A.	7	1898	Eugene E. Keech to J. A. Graves, H. W. O'Melveny & J. H. Shankland
	Graves, Jackson A.	7	1898	Marble & Phibbs to J. A. Graves, H. W. O'Melveny & J. H. Shankland

Subject Hdgs./ Subdivision	*Collection*	*Box*	*Date*	*Finder's Aid*
ESTATES (cont.)				
	Haight, Henry	5	1867	Joseph B. Wells Estate, Haight notes
	Haight, Henry	5	1868	Charles Sawyer to Henry Haight
	Haight, Henry	6	1871	Daniel B. Gale to Henry Haight
	Haight, Henry	2	1852	Ralston and Sunderland to Thomas Fiske
	Haight, Henry	2	1854	Frank O. Day to Joseph Wells
	Jones, Elbert P.	1	1851-65	Elbert Jones Estate Papers
	Keller, Matthew	1	1881-90	Various Keller, Matthew Estate Papers
	Leidesdorff, William A.	5	1848	Leidesdorff Estate Papers
	McCullough, S. L. B.	1	1873	McCullough to Samuel Baker
	New Almaden Mine	1	1864	Estate of John Bowie Gray, Claim
	Shorb, James de Barth	63	1904	Eugene E. Keech to James M. Allen
	Shorb, James de Barth	74	1890	Jefferson Martinet to James de Barth Shorb (various)
	Shorb, James de Barth	75	1891-92	Henry E. Matthews to James de Barth Shorb (various)
	Shorb, James de Barth	83	1891	J. S. Noyes to James de Barth Shorb
	Shorb, James de Barth	91	1897-00	George Smith to Isaias Hellman (various)
	Shorb, James de Barth	93	1889-90	Leonard H. Pockman to James de Barth Shorb (various)
	Shorb, James de Barth	125	1899	Edward L. Watkins to Maria Shorb
	Shorb, James de Barth	129	1886-90	Lewis P. Wiel to James de Barth Shorb (various)

Subject Hdgs./ Subdivision	*Collection*	*Box*	*Date*	*Finder's Aid*
ESTATES (cont.)				
	Stanton, Philip Ackley	1	1928-29	Lothian Estate Papers
	Wolfskill, Lewis	1	1863-66	David Burris Estate Papers
	Wolfskill, Lewis	6	1877	Francois Pioche estate paper
	Woodworth, Selim E.	1	1865-69	Frederick A. Woodworth estate papers
	Graves, Jackson A.	5	1897	Isaias Hellman to J. A. Graves
Banking	Graves, Jackson A.	4	1896	A. F. Morrison to H. W. O'Melveny
Bankruptcy	Graves, Jackson A.	10	1900	Title Insurance & Trust Co. to Graves, O'Melveny and Shankland
Contract	Markham, H. H.	12	1880	H. H. Markham "odd piece" P.S. referencing John D. Bicknell
Creditors	Fernald, Charles	3	1877	E. Fawcett to Charles Fernald
Deed	Fernald, Charles	4	1886	George Biddle to Charles Fernald
Executor	Fernald, Charles	4	1886	George Biddle to Charles Fernald
Guardianship	Fernald. Charles	7	1878	Petition for guardianship of Susana Hill de More
Homestead	Graves, Jackson A.	10	1901	Title Insurance & Trust Co. to H. W. O'Melveny
Mortgage	Graves, Jackson A.	11	1924	Jackson A. Graves to E. S. Pillsbury
Mortgage	Graves, Jackson A.	2	1893	George Peck to Henry O'Melveny
Probate	Fernald, Charles	4	1887	L. C. McKeeby to Charles Fernald
Promissory Note	Graves, Jackson A.	11	1918	Jackson A. Graves to I. W. Hellman
Promissory Note	Graves, Jackson A.	6	1897	Purington & Addair to J. A. Graves

Subject Hdgs./ Subdivision	*Collection*	*Box*	*Date*	*Finder's Aid*
ESTATES (cont.)				
Real Property	Shorb, James de Barth	105	1878	James de Barth Shorb to Prudent Beaudry (various)
Taxation	Fernald, Charles	4	1885	Henry Newhall to Charles Fernald
Trust	Fernald, Charles	8	1883	Rancho Ojai
Trust	Shorb, James de Barth	115	1910	Raymond W. Stephens to Maria Shorb
Trust	Stimson, Marshall	1	1847-51	Culbertson Trust
Will	Fernald, Charles	3	1871	Adam R. Magraw to Fernald & Richards (various)
Will	Fernald, Charles	4	1885	I. C. McKeeby to Charles Fernald
Will	Graves, Jackson A.	4	1896	Porter Brother Co to J. A. Graves
Will	Markham, H. H.	2	1897	Elizabeth Brown to H. H. Markham
Will	Shorb, James de Barth	115	1911	Raymond W. Stephens to Maria Shorb
Will	Stimson, Marshall	1	1948	Stimson to Applegate & Deines
Will	Stimson, Marshall	4	1912-14	"The Great Talent Will Contest"
Will	Stimson, Marshall	2	12-14	Patrick Talent Will Case
FAMILY LAW				
	Baldwin, Anita M.	1	1915	Divorce Decree, Anita Baldwin from McClaughry
	Couts, Cave J.	84	1897-99	Divorce of Cave Couts-Elizabeth B. (Clemens) Couts Schrader
	Haight, Henry	6	1875	Separation Agreement of S. C. Hastings and Wife, various
	Houghton, Shrmn O.	1	1854-75	Guardianship papers
	Watkins, Louise Ward	7	1947	Louise Watkins to Mother (various)
	Watkins, Louise Ward	8	1952	Louise Watkins to various

Subject Hdgs./ Subdivision	*Collection*	*Box*	*Date*	*Finder's Aid*
FAMILY LAW (cont.)				
Community Property	Park, Alice Locke	3	1911	William Hard to Alice Park
Community Property	Park, Alice Locke	5	1916	Laura Pettendrigh to Alice Park
Divorce	Markham, H. H.	13	1896	J. L. Murphy to H. H. Makham
Divorce	Park, Alice Locke	1	1905	Alice Park to nation's governors
INSURANCE				
	Chipman-Dwinelle	2	1909	Day Proceedings of Phenix Ins. Co, v. Springfield F. M. Ins. Co.
	Graves, Jackson A.	8	1899	Chichering, Thomas & Gregory to Graves, O'Melveny & Shankland
	Graves, Jackson A.	8	1899	Equitable Life Assurance Co to Graves, O'Melveny & Shankland
	Markham, H. H.	16	1897	Willis J. Shields to H. H. Markham
	Stanton, Philip Ackley	1	1907	Various to Philip Stanton
	Wolfskill, Lewis	5	1875	Various policies on Wolfskill properties
	Wolfskill, Lewis	7	1877	Various fire on Wolfskill bldgs.
	Wolfskill, Lewis	8	1878	Various policies on Wolfskill properties
LABOR				
	Aram, Joseph	1	1894	Joseph Aram to Eugene Aram
	Bowron, Fletcher	2	1947	Bowron to M. E. Tydings
	Bowron, Fletcher	4	1938	George H. Fisher to Mayor Bowron
	Bowron, Fletcher	33	1938	"Against Proposition no. 1"
	Bowron, Fletcher	34	1944	Statement, Prop. 12

Subject Hdgs./ Subdivision	*Collection*	*Box*	*Date*	*Finder's Aid*
LABOR (cont.)				
	Markham, H. H.	16	1890	San Francisco to Typographical Union to H. H. Markham
	Markham, H. H.	20	1894	H. H. Markham to various on railroad strike
	Park, Alice Locke	7	1930	Harvey O'Connor to Alice Park
	Shorb, James de Barth	50	1889	W. F. Green to James de Barth Shorb
	Watkins, Louise Ward	7	1947	Louise Watkins to Mother (various)
Arbitration	Bowron, Fletcher	5	1939	Irving Stalmaster to Bowron National Shoe Service and United Shoe Workers of America #12
LANDLORD & TENANT				
	Adams & Co.	V2, 18	1853	S. F. Daily Herald
	Adams & Co.	1	1853	Woods to Cohen & Co. of North Point Dock Warehouse
	Adams & Co.	1	1853	Woods, Haskell, Hastings, Flint, Flint, Peabody & Cohen & Co.
	Center, John	1	1854-56	Charles Stuart to various parties of a San Francisco brick yard
	Center, John	2	1857-59	Charles Stuart to various of brick yard
	Center, John	2	1857	John Center to Hare & Rymers
	Center, John	3	1859-60	Charles Stuart to Griffith Davis (various)
	Center, John	3	1860	A. E. Head to John Center
	Center, John	5	1860	John Center to L. L. Lefebre of San Francisco tract

Subject Hdgs./ Subdivision	*Collection*	*Box*	*Date*	*Finder's Aid*
LANDLORD & TENANT (cont.)				
	Fernald, Charles	3	1877	H. P. Buell to Charles Fernald
	Fernald, Charles	3	1877	John Howe to Charles Fernald
	Fernald, Charles	4	1890	J. M. Sears to Charles Fernald
	Fernald, Charles	7	1873-83	Five leases (various parties)
	Fernald, Charles	8	1880	Samuel Bancroft to A. S. Rossilson
	Fernald, Charles	3	1876	Charles Fernald to Samuel Bancroft
	Fernald, Charles	4	1880	Charles Fernald to Samuel Bancroft
	Graves, Jackson A.	8	1899	Alfred Guillou to J. A. Graves
	Graves, Jackson A.	1	1982	Carlos Olvera to H. W. O.Melveny
	Graves, Jackson A.	5	1896	Maurice Hellman to J. A. Graves, H. W. O'Melveny & J. H. Shankland
	Graves, Jackson A.	3	1895	N. Blackstock to H. W. O'Melveny
	Graves, Jackson A.	3	1895	C. A. Hooper to L. W. Blinn Lumber Co
	Graves, Jackson A.	3	1895	Isaias Hellman to J. A. Graves
	Houghton, Shrmn O.	1	1866	Houghton to Barnes & Moore of Alviso lands in Santa Clara Co.
	Howell, Evelyn L. V.	1	1878	Bancroft Blank Lease #729 (Egan & Soto)
	Howell, Evelyn L. V.	1	1879-83	Various to Howell Land Papers
	Jacks, David	c(3)	1880	W. P. L. Winham to Jacks
	Keller, Matthew	3	1894	Machado & Machado to Henry Keller of Rancho la Ballona
	Leidesdorff, Wm. A.	3	1846	W. A. Leidesdorff
	Leidesdorff, Wm. A.	5	1848	Leidesdorff & United States Army
	Markham, H. H.	5	1897	Charles Davies to H. H. Markham

Subject Hdgs./ Subdivision	*Collection*	*Box*	*Date*	*Finder's Aid*
LANDLORD & TENANT (cont.)				
	Morgan, William Rollin	2	1886	George W. Cox to William Morgan
	O'Farrell, Jasper	1	1856	J. O'Farrell to Wm. D. Palmer & Caleb Bartlett
	Potter, Charles & Isaac	1	1816-26	Cain Irrigation Co. & Pacific Power Corp. (various)
	Potter, Charles & Isaac	6	1905-30	Southern Sierra Power Co. (various)
	Potter, Charles & Isaac	7	1923	Southern Sierra Power Co. (various
	Price, Rodman M.	1	1850	A. M. Van Nostrand to R. M. Price
	Shorb, James de Barth	49	1891	Graves, O'Melveny & Shankland to James de Barth Shorb (legal opinion)
	Shorb, James de Barth	121	1883	J. L. Tucker to James de Barth Shorb
	Wolfskill, Lewis	3	1873	Lewis to Jesus Villalobos
Agriculture	Graves, Jackson A.	88-90 LB	1881	Graves to Thomas Bell
Agriculture	Jacks, David	C2	1878	John Kalar to Jacks
Agriculture	Jacks, David	C(3)	1879	George F. Bodfish to Jacks
Agriculture	Jacks, David	C(3)	1880	R. E. Brown to Jacks
Agriculture	Jacks, David	C(1)	1870	T. R. Hopkins to Jacks
Agriculture	Jacks, David	C1	1879	Martin E. Ward to Jacks
Agriculture	Jacks, David	C(2)	1874	John Chestnut to Jacks
Agriculture	Jacks, David	1	1868	Jasper O'Farrell, Michael Kiernan & James Courtwright

Subject Hdgs./ Subdivision	*Collection*	*Box*	*Date*	*Finder's Aid*
LANDLORD & TENANT (cont.)				
Agriculture	Jacks, David	C2	1878	William B. Unruh to Jacks
	Jacks, David	BII3	1872	Bill from Law Office of Williams and Thornton
Hotel	Jacks, David	C(3)	1879	C. Romie to Jacks
Lease	Jacks, David	C(6)	1888	George F. Bodfish to Jacks
Lease	Jacks, David	BV414	1870	Jacks to Henry Grant
Lease	Jacks, David	BV414	1880	Jacks to Anton Gigling
Lease	Jacks, David	C(2)	1878	H. B. Howard to Jacks
Lease	Jacks, David	BII3	1870	Martinex to Jacks
Lease	Jacks, David	BV414	1860	Jacks & Ashley to Hardy Thompson
Lease	Jacks, David	BV414	1860	Jacks, David J. & D. R. Ashley to H. Thompson
Lease	Jacks, David	BV414	1876	Jacks to O. H. Perry Geo. Carrick and Marrison Blim
Lease	Jacks, David	C7	1889	D. L. Leary to Jacks
Lease	Jacks, David	BV414	1860	Letter from Juan Ramon to Jacks
Lease	Jacks, David	C5	1886	W. P. L. Winham to Jacks
Lease	Shorb, James de Barth	46	1890-91	John M. Fuqua to James de Barth Shorb (various)
Lease	Jacks, David	BV414	1870	Jacks to Domingo Prjol; modify Bancroft blank lease
Mining	Barclay, Henry	2	1905	Standard Gold Mining Co. to William O. Andrew
Mining	Barclay, Henry	2	1908	Standard Gold Mining Co. to William Haight
Oil	Fernald, Charles	4	1887	W. L. Hardison to Charles Fernald
Oil	Fernald, Charles	4	1885	Henry Newhall to Charles Fernald
Oil	Fernald, Charles	4	1885	W. L. Hardison to Charles Fernald

Subject Access Guide

Subject Hdgs./ Subdivision	*Collection*	*Box*	*Date*	*Finder's Aid*
LANDLORD & TENANT (cont.)				
Oil	Fernald, Charles	4	1886	W. L. Hardison to Charles Fernald
Promissory Note	Jacks, David	C2	1878	Wm. B. Unruh to Jacks
Public Utility	Potter, Chas & Isaac	5	1923	Nevada-Calif. Electric Co. (various)
Rent	Adams & Co Scrapbk	V1, p. 62	1853	Newspaper Article
Rent	Jacks, David	C8	1890	Mrs. W. Harrison to Jacks
Rent	Jacks, David	V414	1879	Jacks to Ah Jim & Ah Kong
Rent	Jacks, David	V414	1881	Jacks to P. Jorgensen
Rent	Jacks, David	C1	1871	John Iverson to Jacks
Rent	Jacks, David	C5	1886	Jim Kee to Jacks
Rent	Jacks, David	C8	1890	F. Gates to Jacks
Rent	Jacks, David	C6	1887	Mrs. J. J. Collins Gondonin to Mrs. Jacks
Rent	Jacks, David	C3	1880	W. B. Unruh to Jacks
Rent	Jacks, David	BII4	1875	O. H. Perry Account
Rent	Jacks, David	C6	1888	F. Blackin to Jacks
Rent	Jacks, David	C6	1888	L. H. Garrigas to Jacks
Rent	Jacks, David	C7	1889	Paul Talbot to Jacks
Rent	Jacks, David	BII3	1869	Samuel Casiday acct ledger to Jacks
Rent	Jacks, David	BV414	1871	Kennedy, Hopkins & Jacks to Wm. M. R. Parker
Rent	Jacks, David	BV414	1866	Jacks to Gabriel Delonay, Jacks to Henry Olds, Jacks to Daniel Snivdey, Jacks to Chas. McFadden
Rent	Jacks, David	C(3)	1880	C. T. Romie to Jacks

Subject Hdgs./ Subdivision	*Collection*	*Box*	*Date*	*Finder's Aid*
LANDLORD & TENANT (cont.)				
Rent	Jacks, David	BII3	1870	Samuel Casiday acct ledger to Jacks
Rent	Jacks, David	C(1)	1870	Asks Campbell Bros for acctng w/Cassidy
Rent	Jacks, David	BII3	1879	Sheep Account
Rent	Jacks, David	C8	1890	Paul Talbot to Jacks
Rent	Jacks, David	C1	1870	Samuel Cassidy to Jacks
Rent	Jacks, David	BII3	1879	Acc't. by W. H. Clark on Hamilton Property
Rent	Jacks, David	C(2)	1877	A. P. Hendon to Jacks
Rent	Price, Rodman M.	1	1850	R. Price & Augustus Bowie to Thomas H. Bailey
Rent	Price, Rodman M.	1	1850	R. Price & Augustus Bowie to Thomas H. Bailey
Rent	Price, Rodman M.	1	1850	Moffat & Co. to Rodman M. Price & A. G. Abell
Title	Jacks, David	BV414	1876	Jacks to O. H. Perry Geo. Carrick and Marrison Blim
Title	Jacks, David	C7	1889	D. J. Leary to Jacks
Title	Jacks, David	BV414	1860	Letter from Juan Ramon to Jacks
Title	Jacks, David	C5	1886	W. P. L. Winham to Jacks
	Jacks, David	C20	1874	O. H. Perry to Jacks
Water	Barclay, Henry	5	1868	Los Angeles & Water Works of L. A.
Water	Barclay, Henry	5	1868	King, John to D. W. Alexander of Los Angeles Water Works
LAW & PRACTICE				
	Adams & Co.	3	1856	James McDougall to Alfred Cohen

Subject Hdgs./ Subdivision	*Collection*	*Box*	*Date*	*Finder's Aid*
LAW & PRACTICE (cont.)				
	Adams & Co. Coll.	3	1856	Alfred A. Cohen to Samuel M. Wilson
	Adams & Co. Scrpbk.	1(12)	1853	S. F. Herald 12/19/53 notes on buildings
	Adams & Co. Scrpbk.	1(12)	1853	From S. F. Daily Herald 7/28/53 - building
	Adams & Co. Scrpbk.	6	1855	Lists from S. F. Daily Herald
	Aram, Joseph	1	1896	Partnership Agreement of Hunt and Aram
	Bell, Horace	4	1877	Horace Bell to Caroline Rush
	Bell, Horace	2	1904	"The Jews and the Courts"
	Bowron, Fletcher	52	1962	"Legal Aid" by Justin Miller
	Bowron, Fletcher	53	1860-68	L. A. Bar Bulletin (various)
	Center, John	1	1855	William N. Walton to John Center
	Center, John	3	1859	Isaac N. Thorne to John Center
	Center, John	5	1866	Augustus M. Heslep to John Center
	Center, John	5	1867	Samuel Crim to John Center
	Center, John	2	1857	Louis Blanding to John Center
	Center, John	2	1858	John Hastings to John Center
	Center, John	6	1873	Clark Churchill to John Center
	Chipman-Dwinelle	2	1872	Samuel Cassidy to John W. Dwinelle
	Chipman-Dwinelle	1	1872	John W. Dwinelle to Samuel Cassidy
	Chipman-Dwinelle	2	1873	James Green to W. W. Chipman
	Chipman-Dwinelle	4	1861-62	Law Office Day Book
	Chipman-Dwinelle	2	1862	Contract; Jose A. Castro to deed to Hepburn & Fees in land Dwinelle

Subject Hdgs./ Subdivision	*Collection*	*Box*	*Date*	*Finder's Aid*
LAW & PRACTICE (cont.)				
	Chipman-Dwinelle	2	n.d.	William W. Chipman to law firms of Saunders & Hepburn and Shafter, Williams & Park
	Dane Family	1	1854-57	Lawyer's Diary, Sacramento to S.F.
	El Dorado County Arch	IA-6	1850-69	District & County Court records
	Fernald, Charles	1	1856	Gernald to D. K. Ashley
	Fernald, Charles	3	1856	Numa Hubert (S.F. atty) to Charles Fernald
	Fernald, Charles	3	1876	T. J. Gallagher to Charles Fernald (various)
	Fernald, Charles	3	1876	William Webb to Charles Fernald (various)
	Fernald, Charles	3	1877	Albert Dibblee to Charles Fernald (various)
	Fernald, Charles	3	1877	C. W. Goodchild to Charles Fernald
	Fernald, Charles	3	1877	Pringle & Hayne to Charles Fernald (various)
	Fernald, Charles	3	1877	W. T. Maxwell to Charles Fernald
	Fernald, Charles	3	1877	Pringle and Hayne to Charles Fernald (various)
	Fernald, Charles	3	1877	Pringle and Hayne to Charles Fernald (various)
	Fernald, Charles	3	1877	William H. Webb to Charles Fernald (various)
	Fernald, Charles	3	1877	Samuel Wilson to Charles Fernald (various)
	Fernald, Charles	3	1878	O. P. Evans to Charles Fernald (various)

Subject Hdgs./ Subdivision	*Collection*	*Box*	*Date*	*Finder's Aid*
LAW & PRACTICE (cont.)				
	Fernald, Charles	3	1878	Hutton and Godfrey to Charles Fernald (various)
	Fernald, Charles	3	1878	Samuel Wilson to Charles Fernald
	Fernald, Charles	3	1878	James Winans to Charles Fernald (various)
	Fernald, Charles	4	1879	H. G. Newhall to Charles Fernald (various)
	Fernald, Charles	4	1880	Henry E. Highton to Charles Fernald (various)
	Fernald, Charles	4	1880	Surratt & Taylor to Charles Fernald
	Fernald, Charles	4	1880	Robert Crockett to Charles Fernald (various)
	Fernald, Charles	4	1880	Henry Highton to Charles Fernald (various)
	Fernald, Charles	4	1881	B. S. Brooks to Charles Fernald
	Fernald, Charles	4	1881	Pillsbury & Titus to Charles Fernald (various)
	Fernald, Charles	4	1882	B. S. Brooks to Charles Fernald (various)
	Fernald, Charles	4	1883	B. S. Brooks to Charles Fernald
	Fernald, Charles	4	1883	Pillsbury & Titus to Charles Fernald (various)
	Fernald, Charles	4	1884	Henry Newhall to Charles Fernald (various)
	Fernald, Charles	4	1884	H. C. Campbell to Charles Fernald (various)
	Fernald, Charles	4	1887	L. C. McKeeby to Charles Fernald
	Fernald, Charles	4	1890	John J. Boyce to Charles Carrier
	Fernald, Charles	4	1890	Thomas P. Stoney to Charles Fernald (various)

Subject Hdgs./ Subdivision	*Collection*	*Box*	*Date*	*Finder's Aid*
LAW & PRACTICE (cont.)				
	Fernald, Charles	4	1890	Waldo M. York to Charles Fernald
	Fernald, Charles	7	1868-85	Various documents: complaints, answers, cross-complaints, etc.
	Fernald, Charles	3	1876	O. P. Evans to Charles Fernald
	Fernald, Charles	4	1884	James T. Boyd to Charles Fernald
	Graves, Jackson A.	8	1899	James Shankland to J. A. Graves
	Graves, Jackson A.	1	1892	Various to Jackson Graves
	Graves, Jackson A.	1	1892	James Shankland to Jackson Graves
	Graves, Jackson A.	2	1893	Luse & McDonald to Graves, O'Melveny & Shankland
	Graves, Jackson A.	3	1894	E. S. Pillsbury to J. A. Graves
	Graves, Jackson A.	7	1898	Hall McAllister to Henry W. O'Melveny
	Graves, Jackson A.	3	1895	J. S. Chapman to J. A. Graves
	Graves, Jackson A.	3	1895	Wilfred Peck to J. A. Graves, H. W. O'Melveny and Shankland
	Haight, Henry	1	1851	William Root to Henry Haight
	Haight, Henry	2	1852	B. F. Davenport to Henry H. Haight
	Haight, Henry	2	1854	John Heard to Wells, Haight and Gary
	Haight, Henry	2	1854	William Wallace to Wells, Haight and Gary
	Haight, Henry	3	1854	Wallace and Ryland to Wells, Haight & Gary
	Haight, Henry	3	1854	Joseph E. Gary to Henry Haight
	Haight, Henry	3	1854	John Heard to Joseph Wells

Subject Hdgs./ Subdivision	*Collection*	*Box*	*Date*	*Finder's Aid*
LAW & PRACTICE (cont.)				
	Haight, Henry	4	1856	M. A. Mesick to Henry Haight
	Haight, Henry	4	1856	Tweed & Fletcher to Haight & Gary
	Haight, Henry	4	1857	Adolphus Grimwood to Henry Haight
	Halleck, Peachy, Billings	1	1853	Various
	Jones, Elbert P.	1	1854-60	Complaint & Summons
	Markham, H. H.	5	1884	C. D. Daggett to H. H. Markham
	Markham, H. H.	16	1886	Lorenzo Sawyer to H. H. Markham
	Markham, H. H.	16	1886	George Hugh Smith (Glassell, Smith and Patton) to H. H. Markham
	Markham, H. H.	16	1886	Oregon Sanders to H. H. Markham
	Markham, H. H.	19	1884	Byron Waters to H. H. Markham
	Shorb, James de Barth	79	1891	Leroy E. Mosher to James de Barth Shorb
	Shorb, James de Barth	105	1888	James de Barth Shorb to Stephen Johnson Field
	Shorb, James de Barth	81	1886	Francis Newlands to Stephen J. Field regarding Erskine Mayo Ross
	Shorb, James de Barth	49	1885	George G. Goucher to James de Barth Shorb
	Shorb, James de Barth	48	1891	T. E. Gibson to James de Barth Shorb
	Stearns, Abel	17	1855	John B. R. Cooper to Abel Stearns
	Stearns, Abel	27	1852	Stephen C. Foster to Abel Stearns
	Stearns, Abel	33	1852	Henry W. Halleck to Abel Stearns

Subject Hdgs./ Subdivision	Collection	Box	Date	Finder's Aid
LAW & PRACTICE (cont.)				
	Stearns, Abel	35	1852	William P. M. Howard to Abel Stearns
	Stearns, Abel	36	1852	Charles R. Johnson to Abel Stearns
	Stearns, Abel	69	1851	Oliver S. Witherby to Abel Stearns
	Stimson, Marshall	5	1926-50	Stimson Diaries, Dan Books, etc.
	Terry, David Smith	1	1852	David Terry to Cornelia Terry
	Terry, David Smith	3	1870	David Terry to Cornelia Terry
Deed	Fernald, Charles	4	1886	Thomas Dibblee to Charles Fernald
Deed	Leidesdorff, William A.	6	1866	Henry Naglee to D. B. Northrop
Fees	Adams & Co.	4	1858	Samuel Wilson to Alfred Cohen
Fees	Baldwin, Anita M.	5	1897	Bradner W. Lee to H. H. Unruh
Fees	Barclay, Henry	4	1890	James F. Stuart to Barclay & Wilson
Fees	Chipman-Dwinelle	1	1867	John W. Dwinelle to Frank McCoppin & Monroe Asbury
	Chipman-Dwinelle	1	1866	Contract of fee arrangement between William W. Chipman and George E. Whiting
Fees	Graves, Jackson A.	8	1899	T. E. Gibson to Henry O'Melveny
Fees	Graves, Jackson A.	1	1893	Isaias W. Hellman to J. A. Graves
Fees	Leidesdorff, William A.	3	1847	E. P. Jones, contingency fee
Fees	Shorb, James de Barth	134	1891	Langston Winston to N. A. Strain
Fees	Stearns, Abel	10	1867	Montgomery Blair to Fenton M. Slaughter

Subject Hdgs./ Subdivision	*Collection*	*Box*	*Date*	*Finder's Aid*
LAW & PRACTICE (cont.)				
Law Books	Adams & Co. Scrpbk.	1(34)	1853	S. F. Daily Herald; S. F. Law Library
Litigation	Fernald, Charles	3	1877	Joel H. Cooper to Charles Fernald
Litigation	Jacks, David	C(5)	1884	S. O. Houghton to David Jacks
Practice	Fernald, Charles	4	1884	Thomas Bell to Charles Fernald
Procedure	Jacks, David	C(4)	1883	S. O. Houghton to Jacks
Stat. of Lims.	Fernald, Charles	3	1877	John P. Green to Charles Fernald
Stat. of Lims.	Fernald, Charles	3	1878	John P. Green to Charles Fernald
Stat. of Lims.	Graves, Jackson A.	11	1916	Jackson A. Graves to I. W. Hellman
Stat. of Lims.	Graves, Jackson A.	4	1896	League for Better City Government to H. W. O'Melveny
Stat. of Lims.	Graves, Jackson A.	10	1901	Works & Lee to Graves, O'Mel-veny & Shankland
Stat. of Lims.	Graves, Jackson A.	5	1897	A. G. Beyer to J. A. Graves
Stat. of Lims.	Markham, H. H.	7	1890	W. H. Gould to H. H. Markham
Venue	Graves, Jackson A.	9	1900	John G. North to H. W. O'Melveny
Venue	Graves, Jackson A.	4	1896	Fred Button to Henry O'Melveny
Venue	Graves, Jackson A.	7	1898	Hall McAllister to Henry W. O'Melveny
Venue	Graves, Jackson A.	2	1893	A. F. Morrison to Henry O'Melveny
MUNICIPALITIES				
	Bowron, Fletcher	1	1939-41	Bowron to City Council (various)
	Bowron, Fletcher	1	1934	Bowron to City Council (various)
	Bowron, Fletcher	1	1943	Bowron to City Council (various)
	Bowron, Fletcher	1	1944-45	Bowron to City Council (various)
	Bowron, Fletcher	2	1946-48	Bowron to City Council (various)

Subject Hdgs./ Subdivision	*Collection*	*Box*	*Date*	*Finder's Aid*
MUNICIPALITIES (cont.)				
	Bowron, Fletcher	3	1946	Bowron to John G. Mays
	Bowron, Fletcher	3	1948-53	Bowron to City Council (various)
	Bowron, Fletcher	3	1952	Bowron to Herman F. Selvin, Re: *Housing Authority v. L.A.*
	Bowron, Fletcher	34	1943	Address, Lawyer's Club, Nov. 24, 1943
	Bowron, Fletcher	34	1944	"The Problem of the Metropolitan Area"
	Bowron, Fletcher	34	1945-46	Press Releases (various)
	Bowron, Fletcher	35	1946-49	Press Releases, Statements (various)
	Bowron, Fletcher	36	1950-51	Press Releases, Statements (various)
	Bowron, Fletcher	42	1958	"Improved Municipal Government" by Harold W. Kennedy, Co. Counsel
	Bowron, Fletcher	42	1963	Legal Powers... by Harold Kennedy
	Bowron, Fletcher	42	1963	Brown Act by Harold W. Kennedy
	Center, John	2	1857	B. O. Deevoe to John Center
	Center, John	6	1874	Michael Lynch to John Center
	Center, John	6	1877	S. F. Board of Health to John Center (various)
	Crank, James F.	3	1887-91	James Crank to various in 3 Letterbooks
	Fernald, Charles	4	1885	Southern Pacific Co. (various) to Charles Fernald

Subject Hdgs./ Subdivision	*Collection*	*Box*	*Date*	*Finder's Aid*
MUNICIPALITIES (cont.)				
	Ford, John Anson	4	1933-57	Various Los Angeles City Govt. papers incl. charter changes
	Ford, John Anson	32	1935-58	Los Angeles legislation papers
	Ford, John Anson	60	1943-57	Los Angeles legislation papers
	Graves, Jackson A.	9	1900	George Peck to Henry O'Melveny
	Graves, Jackson A.	11	1915	Jackson A. Graves to I. W. Hellman
	Graves, Jackson A.	10	1901	John S. Chapman to Henry O'Melveny
	Graves, Jackson A.	2	1894	H. W. Chynoweth to J. A. Graves, H. W. O'Melveny & J. H. Shankland
	Graves, Jackson A.	4	1896	R. B. Huston to Henry O'Melveny
	Graves, Jackson A.	7	1898	J. W. Pearce to Henry W. O'Melveny
	Graves, Jackson A.	7	1898	James D. Phelan to Henry W. O'Melveny
	Mandeville, James Wylie	4	1854	Charles Scott to James Mandeville
	Mandeville, James Wylie	7	1856	Sewell Knapp to James Mandeville
Airports	Bowron, Fletcher	42	1955	"Legal Aspects of Protecting Airports and Private Property in the Jet Age" by Harold W. Kennedy, County Counsel
Bonds	Graves, Jackson A.	5	1897	Isaias Hellman to J. A. Graves
Recreation	Bowron, Fletcher	42	1957	Law of Recreation by Harold W. Kennedy, County Counsel
Roads	Markham, H. H.	14	80-82	Pendergast, Smith & Co, to Markham, Cogar & Halleck

Subject Hdgs./ Subdivision	*Collection*	*Box*	*Date*	*Finder's Aid*
MUNICIPALITIES (cont.)				
Roads	Markham, H. H.	1	1897	D. W. Lewis (Abstract & Title Co.) to H. H. Markham
Roads	Markham, H. H.	7	1896	Joseph E. Hannon to H. H. Markham
Zoning	Bowron, Fletcher	6	1965	Bowron to Frank P. Doherty
Zoning	Bowron, Fletcher	3	1965	Hingland and Zoning Case (various)
NATURAL RESOURCES				
	Mandeville, James Wylie	2	1853	Samuel Goddard to James Mandeville; title from occupation and use of mining claim
	Mandeville, James Wylie	3	1854	John W. D. Ross to James Mandeville
	Mandeville, James Wylie	4	1854	John W. D. Ross to James Mandeville
	Mandeville, James Wylie	5	1854	Mandeville bull, a. b. 102 (1854) with comment by Alfred Means
	Mandeville, James Wylie	5	1855	B. D. Hyam to James Mandeville
	Mandeville, James Wylie	9	1857	Draft of an "Act for the Encouragement of Quartz Mining"
	Shorb, James de Barth	115	1889	Edward Steele to James de Barth Shorb
Mining	Baker, Robert	1	1878	Edward F. Beale to Robert Baker
Mining	Center, John	2	1857	John Rafael to John Center
Mining	Center, John	4	1863	George Phillips to John Center (various)
Mining	Center, John	4	1863	George Phillips to John Center
Mining	Center, John	6	1875	George Phillips to John Center

Subject Hdgs./ Subdivision	*Collection*	*Box*	*Date*	*Finder's Aid*
NATURAL RESOURCES (cont.)				
Mining	Center, John	4	1863	Abstract of Owens River Mines
Mining	Chipman-Dwinelle	2	1866	Quartz Mining Laws of Nevada Co. & Grass Valley District
Mining	Couts, Cave J.	81-82	1895-41	Land Papers, Ranchito Mine
Mining	Crank, James F.	7	1895	Charles Purdy to W. H. Norway (Gold Bluff Mine in Downieville)
Mining	Crank, James F.	8	1895	Walter Shannon to R. C. Chambers
Mining	El Dorado Cnty Arch	III	1855-83	County mining papers and records
Mining	Graves, Jackson A.	7	1898	Andrew R. Jackson to J. Graves
Mining	Haight, Henry	5	1868	Joseph B. Crockett to Henry Haight
Mining	Hoadley, Milo	1	1863	James Godfrey to Hoadley in Calaveras Co. (others to Hoadley)
Mining	Hoadley, Milo	1	1872	George Treat to Hoadley in various claims
Mining	Keller, Matthew	2	1868	Notice of location, lease, misc. papers
Mining	Keller, Matthew	1	1867	James Hughes to Keller, Matthew of mining claim
Mining	Keller, Matthew	3	1866	Saenz & Saenz to Keller, Matthew of claim in Cuyama Mine
Mining	Kincade, John T.	1	1849-51	Various Kincade to James Kincade
Mining	Mandeville, James Wylie	1	1851	John Campbell conveyance of shares in Wood's Creek claim
Mining	Mandeville, James Wylie	1	1851	Certificate of sale of share of quartz claim by J. D. Smith

Subject Hdgs./ Subdivision	*Collection*	*Box*	*Date*	*Finder's Aid*
NATURAL RESOURCES (cont.)				
Mining	Mandeville, James Wylie	2	1853	Andrew Hatch to James Mandeville
Mining	Mandeville, James Wylie	2	1853	Bill of sale for claim, E. Sawtell to James W. Mandeville
Mining	Mandeville, James Wylie	6	1855	Certificate of sale of mining claim, Alexander Carncross to James Mandeville
Mining	Markham, H. H.	21	1898	Charles Olsen to H. H. Markham
Mining	Markham, H. H.	21	1883	D. R. Dickey to C. H. Walts, etc.
Mining	Markham, H. H.	4	1882	William Clancy to H. H. Markham (various)
Mining	Markham, H. H.	5	1897	Derereaux to H. H. Markham
Mining	Markham, H. H.	4	1890	Thomas Corwin to H. H. Markham
Mining	Markham, H. H.	1	1887	Died Bahten to H. H. Markham (various)
Mining	Markham, H. H.	1	1890	Rhodes & Barstow to H. H. Markham
Mining	Morgan, William Rollin	1	1876	Charles Hendel to Mina Morgan
Mining	Morgan, William Rollin	2	1882	Daniel Titus to William Morgan
Mining	Morgan, William Rollin	2	1886	George W. Cox to William Morgan
Mining	New Almaden Mine	1	1853	John Gray to John Middleton, transfer of interests in mine
Mining	Potter, Charles & Isaac	1	1919	J. S. Cain (Bodie, CA) (various)
Mining	Shorb, James de Barth	78	1894	Henry Mosgrove to James de Barth Shorb
Mining	Shorb, James de Barth	96	1889-91	John Quinn to James de Barth Shorb (various)

Subject Hdgs./ Subdivision	*Collection*	*Box*	*Date*	*Finder's Aid*
NATURAL RESOURCES (cont.)				
Mining	Wolfskill, Lewis	3	1873	Notice of claim in Tujunga Canyon
Mining	Wolfskill, Lewis	3	1873	Notice of claim "Lode de las Animas" in L. A. Co.
Mining	Woodworth, Selim E.	4	1860-64	Woodworth Mining papers (Blue Wing Quartz Mine, Calaveras Co.)
Oil	Aram, Joseph	1	1901	Notices of Claims
Oil	Baker, Robert	4	1897	Sanford Lyon to Robert Baker (various)
Oil	Baker, Robert	3	1879	Robert Baker to Sanford Lyon
Oil	Baker, Robert	3	1879	Sanford Lyon to Robert Baker (various)
Oil	Baker, Robert	4	1879	Charles Forbes to Robert Baker
Oil	Baker, Robert	4	1879	Alvarez & Castillo to Robt. Baker, Piru Oil Claim
Oil	Baker, Robert	4	1879	John Griffith to S. P. Christy, Roblarcito Oil Claim
Oil	Baker, Robert	4	1879	Henry Lubbock to S. P. Christy, San Francisco Oil Claim
Oil	Baker, Robert	4	1879	William Phillips to S. P. Christy, Santa Clara Oil Claim
Oil	Baker, Robert	4	1879	Albert Ruxton to Robert Baker
Oil	Baker, Robert	4	1879	Edward Beale Memorandum: Pico Oil Claim
Oil	Baker, Robert	4	1881	Edward Beale to Robert Baker
Oil	Baker, Robert	4	1881	John Wise to Robert Baker (various)
Oil	Baker, Robert	5	1882	D. G. Scofield to Robert Baker

Subject Hdgs./ Subdivision	Collection	Box	Date	Finder's Aid
NATURAL RESOURCES (cont.)				
Oil	Baker, Robert	1	1866	Chrisher Leaming to E. F. Beale re: San Fernando Petroleum Dist.
Oil	Baker, Robert	1	1877	D. G. Scofield to Beale & Baker
Oil	Baker, Robert	1	1877	Notice of Oil Claim
Oil	Baker, Robert	1	1877	John Wise to R. S. Baker
Oil	Baker, Robert	2	1878	Stanford Lyon to Robert S. Baker (various)
Oil	Baker, Robert	1	1877	Baker, Robert & Pio Pico
Oil	Baker, Robert	4	1880	Various deeds, San Francisco, Baker Oil Claims, documents
Oil	Baker, Robert	5	1883	Wise to Baker Deed to several oil companies
Oil	Baker, Robert	5	1883	Lockwood to Baker deed to Lockwood oil claim
Oil	Baker, Robert	5	1883	Deeds to various oil claims
Oil	Baker, Robert	2	1878	Petra S. Gelach to Baker, Robert San Fernando Oil Claim
Oil	Baker, Robert	2	1879	Sanford Lyon to R. S. Baker
Oil	Baldwin, Anita M.	5	1908	H. A. Unruh to C. A. Canfield
Oil	Bard, Thomas R.	12C	1882-88	Bard & Perkins papers
Oil	Bard, Thomas R.	V(B)	1873-05	Charles Fernald correspondence
Oil	Bard, Thomas R.	I-IV	1865-15	Bard business papers (139 boxes, 9 vol letters to Union Oil, etc., 134 other vol. = 40,000 items)
Oil	Fernald, Charles	2	1880-90	Thomas Bard to Fernald (various)

Subject Hdgs./ Subdivision	*Collection*	*Box*	*Date*	*Finder's Aid*
NATURAL RESOURCES (cont.)				
Oil	Fernald, Charles	2	1891	Thomas Bard to Fernald (various), Union Oil of Cal. matters
Oil	Fernald, Charles	5	1888	Charles Fernald to Thomas Bard (various)
Oil	Ford, John Anson	9	1936-57	Los Angeles oil industry papers
Oil	Graves, Jackson A.	11	1918	Jackson A. Graves to I. W. Hellman
Oil	Graves, Jackson A.	9	1900	Odes Granages to H. W. O'Melveny
Oil	Graves, Jackson A.	9	1900	J. A. Graves to H. H. Shankland, H. W. O'Melveny, Haas, Perry & Hellman
Oil	Graves, Jackson A.	9	1900	A. F. Morrison to Henry W. O'Melveny
Oil	Graves, Jackson A.	11	1916	Jackson A. Graves to I. W. Hellman
Oil	Graves, Jackson A.	11	1917	Jackson A. Graves to I. W. Hellman
Oil	Graves, Jackson A.	11	1917	Jackson A. Graves to I. W. Hellman
Oil	Graves, Jackson A.	11	1919	Jackson A. Graves to I. W. Hellman
Oil	Graves, Jackson A.	10	1901	Joshua Gabbey to Henry O'Melveny
Oil	Graves, Jackson A.	8	1899	Standard Oil Co to J. A. Graves
Oil	Graves, Jackson A.	8	1900	California Star Oil Works Co to Graves, O'Melveny & Shankland
Oil	Graves, Jackson A.	4	1896	Abe Hass to J. A. Graves
Oil	Graves, Jackson A.	5	1897	A. G. Hubbard to J. A. Graves
Oil	Graves, Jackson A.	6	1897	E. S. Pillsbury to J. A. Graves
Oil	Graves, Jackson A.	4	1896	Graves, O'Melveny & Shankland to Sunset Oil Co.

Subject Hdgs./ Subdivision	Collection	Box	Date	Finder's Aid
NATURAL RESOURCES (cont.)				
Oil	Graves, Jackson A.	8	1899	Azro N. Lewis to J. A. Graves
Oil	Keller, Matthew	1	1865	William Bracken to L. A. Pioneer Oil Co.
Oil	Stimson, Marshall	1	1945	Stimson to Harold Ickes
Oil	Stimson, Marshall	1	1943-46	Stimson to various
Oil	Stimson, Marshall	1	1951	Stimson to Cal. Div. of Oil and Gas
Promissory Note	Baker, Robert	1	1877	Baker, Robert & Arcadia Baker to Calvin Paige & Alfred Robinson
PATENT LAW				
	Shorb, James de Barth	33	1885	Charles Crocker to James de Barth Shorb
	Shorb, James de Barth	36	1885-94	Dewey & Co. to James de Barth Shorb (various)
	Shorb, James de Barth	50	1886-87	Will S. Green to James de Barth Shorb
	Shorb, James de Barth	98	1892	William Robinson to James de Barth Shorb
	Shorb, James de Barth	79	1891	Leroy E. Mosher to James de Barth Shorb
	Shorb, James de Barth	124	1886-87	W. N. Walton to Will S. Green and James de Barth Shorb (various)
PUBLIC UTILITIES				
	Graves, Jackson A.	8	1899	San Gabriel Electric Co. to J. A. Graves
	Graves, Jackson A.	8	1899	Robert Bulla to H. W. O'Melveny
	Graves, Jackson A.	7	1898	A. C. Balch (San Gabriel Electric Co.) to Henry W. O'Melveny
	Potter, Charles & Isaac	4	1916	Isaas B. Potter to Charles F. Potter (various)

Subject Hdgs./ Subdivision	*Collection*	*Box*	*Date*	*Finder's Aid*
PUBLIC UTILITIES (cont.)				
	Potter, Charles & Isaac	6	1918-24	Charles F. Potter Correspondence (various)
	Potter, Charles & Isaac	6	1918	The Southern Sierras Power Co. (various)
	Potter, Charles & Isaac	6	1918	Bishop Light & Power Co. (various)
RAILROAD				
	Crank, James F.	2	1885-87	James Crank to various in Letterbooks
	Crank, James F.	3	1887-89	James Crank to various in Letterbooks
	Crank, James F.	3	1890-91	James Crank to various in Letterbook & Pac. Ry. Co. Letterbook
	Crank, James F.	4	1892	James Crank to W. C. Goudy
	Crank, James F.	4	1891-93	James Crank to various in 2 Letterbooks
	Fernald, Charles	4	1886	Charles Crocker to Charles Fernald (various)
	Graves, Jackson A.	10	1901	F. A. Hihn to J. A. Graves
	Graves, Jackson A.	10	1901	San Pedro, Los Angeles & Salt Lake Railroad Co. to J. A. Graves
	Graves, Jackson A.	1	1893	W. P. Gardiner to Henry O'Melveny
	Graves, Jackson A.	2	1893	Jerome Madden to J. A. Graves
	Graves, Jackson A.	5	1896	Southern Pacific RR to J. A. Graves, H. W. O'Melveny & J. H. Shankland
	Graves, Jackson A.	7	1898	R. H. F. Variel to Henry O'Melveny

Subject Hdgs./ Subdivision	Collection	Box	Date	Finder's Aid
RAILROAD (cont.)				
	Haight, Henry	6	1870	Edward Tomkins to Henry Haight
	Jacks, David	C(2)	1874	John T. Wilson to David J. Jacks
	Markham, H. H.	6	1896	T. W. Eby to H. H. Markham
	Railroadiana	1	1879	Legal opinion & docs.
	Shorb, James de Barth	12	1887	August J. Bowie to Electric Improvement Co.
	Shorb, James de Barth	20	1883-87	Central Pacific Railroad Co. to James de Barth Shorb (various)
	Shorb, James de Barth	68	1884	A. H. Lightfoot to James de Barth Shorb
	Shorb, James de Barth	101	1887-92	San Gabriel Valley Rapid Transit Railway to various
	Shorb, James de Barth	112	1889	Southern Pacific Co. to Evan J. Coleman
	Shorb, James de Barth	112	1886-94	Southern Pacific Co. to James de Barth Shorb (various)
	Shorb, James de Barth	117	1887-92	Francis Q. Story to James de Barth Shorb (various)
	Shorb, James de Barth	118	1888	Sunset Transfer Co. to Southern Pacific Co.
	Shorb, James de Barth	112	1889	Southern Pacific Co. to Evan J. Coleman
	Shorb, James de Barth	112	1886-94	Southern Pacific Co. to James de Barth Shorb (various)
	Shorb, James de Barth	117	1887-92	Francis Q. Story to James de Barth Shorb (various)
	Shorb, James de Barth	118	1888	Sunset Transfer Co. to Southern Pacific Co.

Subject Access Guide

Subject Hdgs./ Subdivision	*Collection*	*Box*	*Date*	*Finder's Aid*
RAILROAD (cont.)				
	Shorb, James de Barth	135	1885	Frederick W. Wood to James de Barth Shorb
	Shorb, James de Barth	136	1887	Frederick W. Wood to James de Barth Shorb (various)
Contract	Graves, Jackson A.	5	1896	Southern Pacific RR to J. A. Graves, H. W. O'Melveny & J. H. Shankland
Eminent Domain	Fernald, Charles	4	1887	Charles Crocker to Charles Fernald
	Shorb, James de Barth	123	1879	William R. Wallace to Stephen J. Field
Rates	Graves, Jackson A.	9	1900	W. A. Day to H. W. O'Melveny
Rates	Graves, Jackson A.	9	1900	W. R. Morrison to H. W. O'Melveny
Rates	Graves, Jackson A.	9	1900	Southern Pacific Co to H. W. O'Melveny
Rates	Graves, Jackson A.	10	1901	Frank Lyon to H. W. O'Melveny
Rates	Graves, Jackson A.	10	1901	Southern Pacific Co to H. W. O'Melveny
Rates	Shorb, James de Barth	105	1887	James de Barth Shorb to Centra Pacific Railroad
Real Property	Graves, Jackson A.	10	1901	Southern Pacific Co to J. A. Graves regarding Guadalasca Rancho
Real Property	Graves, Jackson A.	5	1896	Southern Pacific RR to J. A. Graves, H. W. O'Melveny & J. H. Shankland
Real Property	Graves, Jackson A.	5	1896	Stephen White to J. A. Graves

Subject Hdgs./ Subdivision	*Collection*	*Box*	*Date*	*Finder's Aid*
RAILROAD (cont.)				
Real Property	Graves, Jackson A.	4	1895	Southern Pacific RR to J. A. Graves, H. W. O'Melveny & J. H. Shankland
Real Property	Shorb, James de Barth	20	1882	Central Pacific Railroad Co. Law Dept. to Jerome Madden
REAL PROPERTY				
	Azusa-Foothill Cit.	1	1870-91	Abstract of title, Rancho Azusa
	Azusa-Foothill Cit.	1	1889-95	Azusa Deed Book
	Bacon, Henry Douglas	38-41	1860-90	Marengo Rancho papers
	Baker, Robert	3	1879	Charles Polhemus to R. S. Baker
	Baker, Robert	4	1879	Charles Forbes to Baker, Robert
	Baker, Robert	5	1882	Laguna Rancho Lease
	Baker, Robert	5	1882	C. H. Simpkins to Baker, Robert
	Baker, Robert	1	1866	George Hubbell affidavit, Rancho Sobrante San Jacinto
	Baker, Robert	1	1877	C. B. Polhemus to R. S. Baker
	Baker, Robert	1	1877	Ranchi Jurupa papers (various)
	Baldwin, Anita M.	5	1908	H. A. Unruh to C. A. Canfield
	Baldwin, Anita M.	5	1898	H. A. Unruh to Mr. Capitaine
	Baldwin, Anita M.	5	1897	Stephen M. White to H. A. Unruh
	Bard, Thomas R.	1-3	1890-23	Thomas Bard correspondence
	Bard, Thomas R.	14A	1868-11	Calleguas Rancho papers
	Bard, Thomas R.	14B	1893	Conejo Rancho papers
	Bard, Thomas R.	20E	1874	San Francisco Rancho
	Bard, Thomas R.	V(A)	1869-75	Fernald & Richards correspondence

Subject Hdgs./ Subdivision	*Collection*	*Box*	*Date*	*Finder's Aid*
REAL PROPERTY (cont.)				
	Bell, Horace	4	1869	Horace Bell to Caroline Rush
	Bell, Horace	4	1872	Horace Bell to Caroline Rush
	Brent, Joseph	1	1851	Joseph L. to Edward Brent 4/16
	Brent, Joseph	2	1868	Benjamin D. Wilson to Joseph L. Brent, Sale of Rancho Morengo
	Brent, Joseph	3	1871	Wilson, Benjamin to Joseph Brent
	Brent, Joseph	3	1876	Watkins, Edward to Joseph Brent
	Center, John	1	1855	William N. Walter to John Center
	Center, John	5	1867	Samuel Crim to John Center
	Center, John	5	1869	William Thompson to John Center
	Center, John	6	1876	James Houston to John Center
	Center, John	2	1858	J. T. Stocker to John Center
	Center, John	2	1858	J. T. Stocker to John Center (various)
	Center, John	4	1863	Nicholas Smith to John Center
	Center, John	5	1869	E. Caldwell to John Center
	Center, John	3	1859	William Corbett to John Center
	Chipman-Dwinelle	1	1871	Warren F. Sexton to William W. Chipman
	Chipman-Dwinelle	1	1867	Rancho Encinal San Antonio Litigation file
	Chipman-Dwinelle	1	1854-16	Litigation Papers, Various Alameda County Properties
	Chipman-Dwinelle	1	1866	Deeds: Rancho Jesus de Maria

Subject Hdgs./ Subdivision	Collection	Box	Date	Finder's Aid
REAL PROPERTY (cont.)				
	Chipman-Dwinelle	1	1879	Abstract of Title to Tulare Co. Land to Alfred Daggett
	Chipman-Dwinelle	1	1869-72	Deeds to Tulare Co. Lands acquired by John Whipple Dwinelle
	Chipman-Dwinelle	1	1868	Deed: Sonoma Co., Ralph Harrison to John W. Powell
	Chipman-Dwinelle	1	1869	Deed: San Diego Co. land acquired by John Whipple Dwinelle
	Chipman-Dwinelle	1	1869-72	Deeds: Kern Co. lands acquired by John Whipple Dwinelle
	Chipman-Dwinelle	1	1884	Abstract of Title to land in Contra Costa Co. for E. F. Pierce
	Chipman-Dwinelle	1	1879-96	Deeds: Alameda Co. lands acquired by Caroline E. Chipman Dwinelle
	Chipman-Dwinelle	1	1857-73	Deeds: Various Alameda Co. lands acquired by Chipman Family
	Chipman-Dwinelle	1	1851-55	Litigation Papers: Alameda Co.
	Chipman-Dwinelle	1	1880	Litigation Papers: Alameda Co.
	Chipman-Dwinelle	2	1869-96	Various land papers
	Chipman-Dwinelle	2	1913	Deed: Fannie Chipman to W. F. Chipman, land in Alameda
	Chipman-Dwinelle	1	1873-74	Various Dwinelle School Land Papers
	Chipman-Dwinelle	2	1872	G. W. Hanley to J. W. Dwinelle

Subject Hdgs./ Subdivision	*Collection*	*Box*	*Date*	*Finder's Aid*
REAL PROPERTY (cont.)				
	Chipman-Dwinelle	2	1862	Sale of Mining Claims to Charles Marshall, Holcomb Valley District
	Chipman-Dwinelle	2	1861-65	Daniel Siel Deed, etc. San Francisco land
	Chipman-Dwinelle	2	1920	Various Alameda Co. Land Papers
	Chipman-Dwinelle	2	1907	Abstract of Title to Rancho Encinal de San Antonio
	Couts, Cave J.	75	1859-30	Rancho Agua Hedionda Papers
	Couts, Cave J.	75	1845-96	Rancho Buena Vista Papers
	Couts, Cave J.	76	1897-07	Rancho Buena Vista Papers
	Couts, Cave J.	77	1875	Rancho Cajon Papers
	Couts, Cave J.	77	1892-26	Rancho Guajome Papers
	Couts, Cave J.	77	1898	Rancho La Joya Papers
	Couts, Cave J.	77	1832	Rancho Monserrate Papers
	Couts, Cave J.	77	1890	Rancho La Nacion Papers
	Couts, Cave J.	77	1864	Rancho San Francisco (San Diego County) Papers
	Couts, Cave J.	78	1904	Rancho Santa Margarita y Las Flores Papers
	Couts, Cave J.	78	1876	Rancho Temecula papers
	Couts, Cave J.	78	1870	Rancho Valle de San Jose and Valle de Pamp
	Couts, Cave J.	78	1873-88	Land Papers, Coronado
	Couts, Cave J.	78	1932-39	Land Papers, Fallbrook
	Couts, Cave J.	78	1916-42	Land Papers, Los Angeles

Subject Hdgs./ Subdivision	*Collection*	*Box*	*Date*	*Finder's Aid*
REAL PROPERTY (cont.)				
	Couts, Cave J.	78	1925	Land Papers, Moosa
	Couts, Cave J.	78	1885-39	Land Papers, Oceanside
	Couts, Cave J.	78	1887-00	Land Papers, La Presa
	Couts, Cave J.	78-79	1850	Land Papers, San Diego
	Couts, Cave J.	79	1912-18	Land Papers, Vista
	Couts, Cave J.	80	1890-98	Land Papers, San Bernardino Co.
	Crank, James F.	11	1882-02	Misc. legal papers incl. deed, title opinions, etc.
	Crank, James F.	2	1881-87	James Crank to various in Letterbooks
	Crank, James F.	3	1887-89	James Crank to various in Letterbook
	Crank, James F.	3	1890-91	James Crank to various in 2 Letterbooks
	Crank, James F.	4	1896	James Crank to P. A. Demens
	Crank, James F.	5	1896	John D. Bickness to James Crank
	Crank, James F.	9	1877-92	Fair Oaks Ranch (Pasadena) Land Papers incl. notes on boundaries and transactions
	Crank, James F.	9	1843-77	Abstract to Fair Oaks Ranch (Pasadena)
	Dalton, Henry	5	1865	Edward J. Pringle to Henry Dalton (various)
	Dalton, Henry	5	1865	Henry Dalton to Edward J. Pringle (various)
	Dalton, Henry	5	1865	Henry Dalton to Pioche & Bayerque
	Dalton, Henry	5-7	1865-76	Lester L. Robinson to Henry Dalton (various)

Subject Hdgs./ Subdivision	*Collection*	*Box*	*Date*	*Finder's Aid*
REAL PROPERTY (cont.)				
	Dalton, Henry	5-6	1866-69	Henry Dalton to Lester L. Robinson (various)
	Dalton, Henry	6-7	1869-71	Edmond L. Gould to Henry Dalton (various)
	Dalton, Henry	7	1872	John B. Felton to Henry Dalton
	Dalton, Henry	7	1874	Henry Dalton to John B. Felton
	Dalton, Henry	8	1878	Henry Dalton to Mullan and Hyde
	Dalton, Henry	8	1880	Lynde & Hough to Henry Dalton
	Dalton, Henry	9-10	1880-83	John Mullan to Henry Dalton (various)
	Dalton, Henry	9	1881	Sir Edward Thornton to John Mullan
	Dalton, Henry	10	1881	William L. Booker to Henry Dalton
	Dalton, Henry	10	1883	Henry Dalton to Charles Crocker
	Dalton, Henry	5-7	1866-76	Lester L. Robinson to Henry Dalton (various)
	Dalton, Henry	6	1867	John T. Worner to Lester L. Robinson
	Dalton, Henry	6	1867	Henry Dalton to Lester Robinson
	Dalton, Henry	7	1873-74	Winnall A. Dalton to Henry Dalton (various)
	Dalton, Henry	8	1879-80	John Mullan to Henry Dalton (various)
	Dalton, Henry	8	1880	Henry Dalton to John Mullan
	Dalton, Henry	9	1880	Williamson to Henry Beard
	Dalton, Henry	13	1840-80	Rancho San Jose Land Papers
	Dalton, Henry	13	1842	Land Grant to Zamorano

Subject Hdgs./ Subdivision	Collection	Box	Date	Finder's Aid
REAL PROPERTY (cont.)				
	Dalton, Henry	13	1845-73	Rancho San Francisquito Land Papers
	Dalton, Henry	13	1852	Various Land Papers of Dalton
	Dalton, Henry	13	1869	Mission San Diego Land Papers
	Dalton, Henry	14	1841	Land Grant, Rancho Azusa Duarte
	Dalton, Henry	14	1841-84	Rancho Azusa Land papers incl. land claims litigation
	Dalton, Henry	14	1856-81	Various land claims actions of Henry Dalton
	Dalton, Henry	14	1879	Mullan & Hyde brief in Rancho Azusa land claim litigation
	Dane Family	1	1898	Joseph Berlin to Lois Dane
	El Dorado County Arch	IB1-3	1871-92	County Land Records incl. land claims and locations
	Fernald, Charles	3	1868	John P. Green to Charles Fernald
	Graves, Jackson A.	2	1894	Chino Valley Beet Sugar Co to H. W. O'Melveny
	Graves, Jackson A.	3	1895	Carlos Olvera to H. W. O'Melveny
	Graves, Jackson A.	79-80-LB	1879	J. A. Graves to C. S. Andrews
	Graves, Jackson A.	9	1900	Carlos Olvera to H. W. O'Melveny
	Graves, Jackson A.	11	1914	Jackson A. Graves to I. W. Hellman
	Graves, Jackson A.	11	1916	Jackson A. Graves to I. W. Hellman
	Graves, Jackson A.	11	1917	Jackson A. Graves to I. W. Hellman
	Graves, Jackson A.	11	1917	Jackson A. Graves to I. W. Hellman
	Graves, Jackson A.	11	1919	Jackson A. Graves to I. W. Hellman

Subject Hdgs./ Subdivision	*Collection*	*Box*	*Date*	*Finder's Aid*
REAL PROPERTY (cont.)				
	Graves, Jackson A.	10	1901	Carlos Olvera to H. W. O'Melveny
	Graves, Jackson A.	10	1901	Louis Sloss & Co to J. A. Graves
	Graves, Jackson A.	8	1900	Cave Couts to J. A. Graves
	Graves, Jackson A.	8	1899	Isaias Hellman to J. A. Graves
	Graves, Jackson A.	8	1899	Carlos Olvera to H. W. O'Melveny
	Graves, Jackson A.	8	1899	W. A. Driscoll to J. A. Graves, H. O'Melveny & Shankland
	Graves, Jackson A.	8	1899	Wood & Church to J. A. Graves
	Graves, Jackson A.	8	1899	Cave Couts to J. A. Graves
	Graves, Jackson A.	1	1892	Leon Moss to Graves, O'Melveny & Shankland
	Graves, Jackson A.	1	1892	N. Ohlandt & Co to H. W. O'Melveny
	Graves, Jackson A.	2	1893	N. Ohlandt & Co to H. W. O'Melveny
	Graves, Jackson A.	3	1895	Entler & Obear to J. A. Graves
	Graves, Jackson A.	3	1895	Isaias Hellman to J. A. Graves
	Graves, Jackson A.	2	1894	Courtney Clark to J. A. Graves
	Graves, Jackson A.	3	1894	S. D. Rosenbaum to J. A. Graves
	Graves, Jackson A.	3	1894	Maria Jesus de Shorb to H. W. O'Melveny
	Graves, Jackson A.	2	1894	Frank King to Graves
	Graves, Jackson A.	2	1894	F. A. Hyde to H. W. O'Melveny
	Graves, Jackson A.	2	1894	Carlos Olvera to H. W. O'Melveny
	Graves, Jackson A.	5	1896	A. S. Kimball to J. A. Graves (various)

Subject Hdgs./ Subdivision	Collection	Box	Date	Finder's Aid
REAL PROPERTY (cont.)				
	Graves, Jackson A.	5	1896	Stephen White to Wm. Kerckhoff
	Graves, Jackson A.	3	1895	Carlos Olvera to H. W. O'Melveny
	Graves, Jackson A.	5	1897	Luis Arques to H. W. O'Melveny
	Graves, Jackson A.	5	1897	Balfour, Guthrie to J. A. Graves, H. W. O'Melveny & J. H. Shankland (various)
	Graves, Jackson A.	5	1897	Chauncey P. Biggs to H. J. O'Melveny
	Graves, Jackson A.	5	1897	Chickering, Thomas & Gregory to J. A. Graves, H. W. O'Melveny & J. H. Shankland
	Graves, Jackson A.	7	1898	Carlos Olvera to Henry W. O'Melveny
	Graves, Jackson A.	7	1898	George H. Peck to Henry W. O'Melveny
	Graves, Jackson A.	7	1898	A. S. Kimball to J. A. Graves
	Graves, Jackson A.	5	1897	R. B. Huston to Henry O'Melveny
	Graves, Jackson A.	6	1897	Carlos Olvera to H. W. O'Melveny
	Haight, Henry	5	1858	Deed: Eugene Sullivan to James Donahue
	Haight, Henry	5	1860	Deed: Wells to Donahue of San Francisco Water Lots
	Haight, Henry	5	1861	Deed: John & Euphemia Snethen to James Donahue, S.F. Water Lots
	Haight, Henry	5	1862	Deed: James Donahue to S.F. Gas Co., Water Lots

Subject Hdgs./ Subdivision	Collection	Box	Date	Finder's Aid
REAL PROPERTY (cont.)				
	Haight, Henry	5	1866	Henry Haight to Eugene Casserly
	Haight, Henry	6	1871	E. O. F. Hastings to Henry Haight
	Haight, Henry	2	1853	Deed to San Francisco Water Lots (various)
	Haight, Henry	2	1854	M. A. Stout to Henry Haight
	Haight, Henry	2	1854	Aylett Buckner to Joseph Wells
	Haight, Henry	3	1854	Benjamin Orrick to Joseph Wells
	Haight, Henry	3	1854	George H. Derby to Joseph Wells
	Haight, Henry	3	1854	Deed: Haight to Wells, Water Lots
	Haight, Henry	3	1854	Deed of Joseph Folsom to S. F. Gas Comapny
	Halleck, Peachy, Billings	2	1861	Halleck to James Mandeville
	Halleck, Peachy, Billings	2	1853	Peachy's memo on Cal. Land Laws
	Hoadley, Milo	1	1871	Augustus Dowd to Hoadley
	Houghton, Shrmn. O.	1	1859	Monterey Pueblo (183) map
	Houghton, Shrmn. O.	1	1866	Rufus Hopklins to Stephen J. Field re: Spanish Archives in Calif.
	Howell, E. L. W.	1	1870	Grant Deeds; form deeds for law firm of Mullan & Hyde; bargain & sale, quitclaims
	Howell, E. L. W.	1	1860-77	Warranty deed
	Jacks, David	C(4)	1881	Goodall Perkins & Co to D Jacks
	Jacks, David	BIII8	1885	William L. Ross declaration of Trust
	Jacks, David	C(2)	1873	M. C. Ireland to David Jacks

Subject Hdgs./ Subdivision	Collection	Box	Date	Finder's Aid
REAL PROPERTY (cont.)				
	Jones, Elbert P.	1	1848-51	Jones Land Papers for San Francisco lots incl. diagrams
	Jones, Elbert P.	1	1868	Michael Burke to Joseph & Sarah Lewis
	Keller, Matthew	3	1874	Handwritten Deed
	Keller, Matthew	3	1877	Warranty Deed, Bargain & Sale Deed
	Keller, Matthew	3	1891-97	Shafer & Shafer to Union Oil
	Leidesdorff, William A.	1	1844	Petronilo Rios' Petition, El Plieto Rancho
	Leidesdorff, William A.	2	1846	Petition of Lazaro Everhart to pio Pico for land grant
	Leidesdorff, William A.	4	1847	Petition to grant Rancho Acalanes to Wm. Leidesdorff
	Leidesdorff, William A.	6	1853	Archibald Peachy to J. L. Folsom (various)
	Leidesdorff, William A.	6	1852	Joseph L. Folsom to Archibald Peachy
	Leidesdorff, William A.	6	1852	John B. Weller to Joseph L. Folsom
	Leidesdorff, William A.	6	1853	Frederick Billings to Joseph L. Folsom
	Leidesdorff, William A.	6	1853	Philip Hamilton to Archibald Peachy
	Leidesdorff, William A.	6	1855	William C. Barron to Archibald Peachy
	Mandeville, James Wylie	3	1854	William Fowler to James Mandeville
	Mandeville, James Wylie	8	1857	M. Wappall to James Mandeville
	Markham, H. H.	10	1890	Frank P. Kelly to H. H. Markham

Subject Hdgs./ Subdivision	*Collection*	*Box*	*Date*	*Finder's Aid*
REAL PROPERTY (cont.)				
	Markham, H. H.	21	1875-93	H. H. Markham (various)
	Morgan, William Rollin	1	1874	George Dodge to William Morgan
	O'Farrell, Jasper	1	1851-55	Jasper O'Farrell to John O'Farrell
	Potter, Charles & Isaac	1	1915	Cain irrigation Co. (various)
	Potter, Charles & Isaac	3	1911	Hillside Water Co. & Nevada-Calif. Power Co.
	Potter, Charles & Isaac	3	1922	Hydro-Electric Co.
	Potter, Charles & Isaac	4	1920	Mono Power Company (various)
	Potter, Charles & Isaac	5	1922-24	The Sierras Construction Co. (various)
	Potter, Charles & Isaac	6	1918	The Southern Sierras Power Co. (various)
	Potter, Charles & Isaac	7	1906	J. M. Elliott, et al. to Bd. of Water Com'rs of L. A. County
	Potter, Charles & Isaac	7	1923	Southern Sierra Power Co. (various)
	Potter, Charles & Isaac	1	1915-33	Cain Irrigation Co. (various)
	Potter, Charles & Isaac	6	1905-30	Southern Sierras Power Co. (various)
	Potter, Charles & Isaac	3	1916-28	Interstate Telegraph Co. (various)
	Shorb, James de Barth	20	1889	Chapman to Hendrick to James de Barth Shorb
	Shorb, James de Barth	7	1883	Henry D. Bacon to James de Barth Shorb
	Shorb, James de Barth	7	1883	Arturo Bandini to James de Barth Shorb

Subject Hdgs./ Subdivision	Collection	Box	Date	Finder's Aid
REAL PROPERTY (cont.)				
	Shorb, James de Barth	10	1890	James H. Benedict to James de Barth Shorb (various)
	Shorb, James de Barth	11	1884	Thomas Benton Bishop to James de Barth Shorb
	Shorb, James de Barth	15	1883	Charles Cabor to James de Barth Shorb
	Shorb, James de Barth	40	1893	Earley & Conger to James de Barth Shorb
	Shorb, James de Barth	41	1887	Asa Ellis to James de Barth Shorb
	Shorb, James de Barth	49	1894	Graces, O'Melveny & Shankland to Maria Shorb
	Shorb, James de Barth	52	1892	William H. Hall to Francis G. Newlands
	Shorb, James de Barth	54	1883	F. C. Hazen to Maria Shorb
	Shorb, James de Barth	60	1891	Stephen C. Hubbell to James de Barth Shorb
	Shorb, James de Barth	63	1883	Gilbert S. Keys to James de Barth Shorb
	Shorb, James de Barth	63	1887	Charles J. King to James de Barth Shorb
	Shorb, James de Barth	106	1878	James de Barth Shorb to Samuel Hubbard
	Shorb, James de Barth	76	1886	Richard Melrose to James de Barth Shorb
	Shorb, James de Barth	91	1885	George Smith Patton to James de Barth Shorb
	Shorb, James de Barth	91	1887	George Smith Patton to James de Barth Shorb
	Shorb, James de Barth	77	1897	Victor Montgomery to Maria Shorb

Subject Hdgs./ Subdivision	*Collection*	*Box*	*Date*	*Finder's Aid*
REAL PROPERTY (cont.)				
	Shorb, James de Barth	78	1887	Henry N. Morgan to James de Barth Shorb
	Shorb, James de Barth	110	1890	Tristram L. Skinner to James de Barth Shorb
	Shorb, James de Barth	119	1875	George Thompson to Glassell, Chapman & Smith
	Shorb, James de Barth	110	1890	Tristram L. Skinner to James de Barth Shorb
	Shorb, James de Barth	119	1876	George Thompson to Glassell, Chapman & Smith
	Shorb, James de Barth	120	1887-88	James M. Tiernan to James de Barth Shorb (various)
	Shorb, James de Barth	123	1887-93	James Vollmar to James de Barth Shorb (various)
	Shorb, James de Barth	131	1868-78	Benjamin D. Wilson to James de Barth Shorb (various)
	Shorb, James de Barth	132	1869-76	Benjamin D. Wilson to Maria Shorb (various)
	Shorb, James de Barth	134	1878	Frederick W. Wood to James de Barth Shorb (various)
	Shorb, James de Barth	135	1885-86	Frederick W. Wood to James de Barth Shorb (various)
	Stearns, Abel	16	1867	A. Chester to Abel Stearns (various)
	Stearns, Abel	16	1867	A. Chester to Isaac Hartman
	Stearns, Abel	16	1867	Cornelius Cole to Abel Stearns
	Stearns, Abel	20	1852	Richard Somerset Den to Abel Stearns
	Stearns, Abel	28	1868	Charles H. Forbes to Abel Stearns (various)

Subject Hdgs./ Subdivision	Collection	Box	Date	Finder's Aid
REAL PROPERTY (cont.)				
	Stearns, Abel	33	1865-68	Isaac Hartman to Matthew Keller (various)
	Stearns, Abel	35	1859	Sidney L. Johnson to Joseph P. Thompson
	Stearns, Abel	35	1864	Sidney L. Johnson to John Parrott
	Stearns, Abel	36-37	1858-62	Charles P. Johnson to Abel Stearns (various)
	Stearns, Abel	38	1853	William Carey Jones to Abel Stearns
	Stearns, Abel	41	1870	Timothy Lynch to Abel Stearns
	Stearns, Abel	47	1864	John Parrott to Abel Stearns
	Stearns, Abel	51	1850-61	Louis de Robidoux to Abel Stearns
	Stearns, Abel	58	1868	Horace to Abel Stearns (various)
	Stearns, Abel	62	1854	Abel Stearns to John C. Fremont
	Stearns, Abel	62	1855	Abel Stearns to John B. Weller
	Stearns, Abel	62	1867	Abel Stearns to Joseph S. Wilson
	Stearns, Abel	64	1854	C. B. Strode to Abel Stearns
	Stearns, Abel	64	1852	Henry F. Teschemacher to Abel Stearns
	Stearns, Abel	67	1856-63	Juan de Toro Correspondence
	Stearns, Abel	68	1868	William Walker correspondence
	Stearns, Abel	68	1834-68	Jonathan Warner correspondence
	Stearns, Abel	68	1854-56	Thomas Warner correspondence
	Stearns, Abel	69	1868	Ivar Weid correspondence
	Stearns, Abel	69	1871	Samuel Woods correspondence
	Stearns, Abel	4	1868	Alexander Badlam correspondence
	Stearns, Abel	10	1856	Matthew Biggs correspondence

Subject Hdgs./ Subdivision	Collection	Box	Date	Finder's Aid
REAL PROPERTY (cont.)				
	Stearns, Abel	11	1868	Calvin Brown correspondence
	Stearns, Abel	12	1856	Samuel Bruce correspondence
	Stearns, Abel	12	1867	Peter Burnett correspondence
	Stearns, Abel	16	1867-73	Moses Cobb correspondence
	Stearns, Abel	18	1851-59	Cave J. Couts correspondence
	Stearns, Abel	19	1861-70	Cave J. Couts correspondence
	Stearns, Abel	27	1847-54	John C. Fremont correspondence
	Stearns, Abel	27	1851	George Gliddon correspondence
	Stearns, Abel	33	1868	G. G. Guild correspondence
	Stearns, Abel	34	1867	E. W. Haskell correspondence
	Stearns, Abel	34	1861-68	William Hollister correspondence
	Stearns, Abel	35	1867	Alfred Jones correspondence
	Stearns, Abel	45	1876	Henry Murray correspondence
	Stearns, Abel	45	1867	J. A. Nicholson correspondence
	Stearns, Abel	47	1868	C. B. R. Painter correspondence
	Stearns, Abel	48	1854	Levi Parsons correspondence
	Stearns, Abel	50	1865	Edward Poole correspondence
	Stearns, Abel	51	1853	Andrew Randall correspondence
	Stearns, Abel	51	1856-58	Encarnacion Robbins correspondence
	Stearns, Abel	54-56	1833-73	Alfred Robinson correspondence
	Stearns, Abel	51	1867	Lester Robinson correspondence
	Stearns, Abel	57	1834-45	Mariano Roldan correspondence
	Stearns, Abel	58	1867	William Rosecrans correspondence
	Stearns, Abel	60	1852	Miguel Smith correspondence

Subject Hdgs./ Subdivision	Collection	Box	Date	Finder's Aid
REAL PROPERTY (cont.)				
	Stearns, Abel	60	1832-68	David Spence correspondence
	Stearns, Abel	63	1867	A. H. Stephens correspondence
	Stearns, Abel	63	1867-68	John D. Stephens correspondence
	Stearns, Abel	63	1846	James Stokes correspondence
	Stearns, Abel	64	1846-54	John A. Sutter correspondence
	Stearns, Abel	64	1849-56	Alexander Taylor correspondence
	Stimson, Marshall	10	1912-41	Various
	Wolfskill, Lewis	1	1862	Homestead declaration of Guadalupe Dalton on Rancho Azusa
	Wolfskill, Lewis	2	1870	Baldwin of Rancho Santa Anita
	Wolfskill, Lewis	2	1872	Decree authorizing Dolores Correa sell L. A. land
	Wolter, Charles	2		Mutual Agreement to sell to lots as single parcel
	Wolter, Charles	1	1848	Deed - Jose M. Escobar to Encainacion Garcia
	Woodworth, Selim E.	1	1841-69	Woodworth land papers
Adverse Possession	Shorb, James de Barth	91	1908	George Smith Patton to Maria Shorb
Attachment	Markham, H. H.	1	1887	Died Bahten to H. H. Markham
Bankruptcy	Jacks, David	C8	1890	W. M. R. Parker to Jacks
Bond	Shorb, James de Barth	64	1895	John C. Kirkpatrick to James de Barth Shorb
Boundaries	Fernald, Charles	4	1884	Robert Harries to Charles Fernald
Boundaries	Fernald, Charles	4	1884	Henry Newhall to Charles Fernald

Subject Hdgs./ Subdivision	*Collection*	*Box*	*Date*	*Finder's Aid*
REAL PROPERTY (cont.)				
Boundaries	Fernald, Charles	5	1891	Alphonso Wigmore to Charles Fernald (various)
Bounty Warrant	Jacks, David	C(3)	1880	David Jacks to James F. Stuart
Chinese Rights	Jacks, David	C5	1886	J. A. Clayton to Jacks
Condemnation	Bowron, Fletcher	3	1952	Memorandum... Herman F. Selvin ...representing Samuel Goldwyn Studios
Condemnation	Potter, Charles & Isaac	4	1920	Los Angeles v. Mono Power Co. (various)
Contract	Baker, Robert	1	1877	Arcadia Baker to Charles Felton re Rancho Jurupa
Contract	Graves, Jackson A.	1	1893	W. P. Gardiner to Henry O'Melveny
Conveyance	Fernald, Charles	4	1881	M. F. Pickering Co. to Charles Fernald (various)
Covenant	Jacks, David	B(V-13)	1890	Deed: Jacks to F. Botsch
Deed	Adams & Co.	3	1856	Palmer to Cohen of S. F. Lot
Deed	Baker, Robert	3	1879	Rancho San Vincente & Santa Monica
Deed	Baker, Robert	5	1882	Julius Christy to John Wise, lands on several counties
Deed	Baker, Robert	1	1877	J. P. Jones & C. S. Baker to George Armstrong
Deed	Baldwin, Anita M.	5	1905	Rancho La Puente
Deed	Barclay, Henry	1	1887	J. W. Reed to Irvington Land & Water Co., San Bernardino, CA
Deed	Barclay, Henry	1	1887	Oliver, S. J. to Irvington Land & Water Co., San Bernardino

Subject Hdgs./ Subdivision	*Collection*	*Box*	*Date*	*Finder's Aid*
REAL PROPERTY (cont.)				
Deed	Barclay, Henry	1	1888	Mills, A. F. to Irvington Land & Water Co., San Bernardino
Deed	Barclay, Henry	1	1890	Irvington Land & Water Co. to M. J. Clapp
Deed	Barclay, Henry	1	1887	Hill, Hiram to Irvington Land & Water Co.
Deed	Barclay, Henry	1	1887	Gay, Leslie to Irvington Land & Water Co.
Deed	Barclay, Henry	1	1887	Fox, C. J. to Irvington Land & Water Co.
Deed	Barclay, Henry	1	1888	Foster, P. G. to Irvington Land & Water Co.
Deed	Barclay, Henry	1	1888	Barrett, C. H. to Irvington Land & Water Co.
Deed	Barclay, Henry	1	1888-97	Henry A. Barclay (various)
Deed	Barclay, Henry	4	1868	Hays, John C. to Andrew J. Pope, Rancho Muscupiabe, San Bernardino
Deed	Barclay, Henry	4	1885	Barclay, F. H. to Irvington Land & Water Co.
Deed	Barclay, Henry	4	1885	Akers, John B. to Wilson, Robert N. C. (Rancho Muscupiabe)
Deed	Bell, Horace	1	1850	Magruder & Sumner to Abel Stearns
Deed	Brent, Joseph	3	1877	Benjamin D. Wilson to Joseph Brent
Deed	Center, John	2	1858	Keller, Matthew to John Center
Deed	Chipman-Dwinelle	1	1866	Bargain & Sale deed form of Wm. B. Cooke & Co., San Francisco

Subject Hdgs./ Subdivision	*Collection*	*Box*	*Date*	*Finder's Aid*
REAL PROPERTY (cont.)				
Deed	Chipman-Dwinelle	Folder 2	1913	Wm. Chipman to Fanny Chipman of Encinal Park Tract
Deed	Fernald, Charles	8	1850	Various regarding the land of the Arellanes, Camarillos, Pietras, & Vidals in Santa Barbara County
Deed	Fernald, Charles	7	1853-89	68 deeds, land papers (various)
Deed	Fernald, Charles	3	1856	John C. Jones to Charles Fernald (various)
Deed	Fernald, Charles	8	1856	Tancho Jonata
Deed	Fernald, Charles	8	1862	Rancho de las Milpitas
Deed	Fernald, Charles	3	1868	John D. Patterson to Charles Fernald (various)
Deed	Fernald, Charles	3	1868	John D. Patterson to Charles Fernald (Rancho Goleta)
Deed	Fernald, Charles	3	1869	J. T. Richards to Charles Fernald
Deed	Fernald, Charles	8	1871	Rancho Conejo
Deed	Fernald, Charles	8	1876	Rancho Temescal
Deed	Fernald, Charles	8	1877-80	Various deed, abstracts of title
Deed	Fernald, Charles	3	1878	Edward Hoar to Charles Fernald
Deed	Fernald, Charles	3	1878	A. W. Thompson to Charles Fernald
Deed	Fernald, Charles	4	1879	H. M. Newhall to Charles Fernald
Deed	Fernald, Charles	4	1881	Horace Hawkes to Charles Fernald
Deed	Fernald, Charles	5	1881	Samuel Backus to Charles Fernald
Deed	Fernald, Charles	5	1881	Charles Fernald to Lazard Freres
Deed	Fernald, Charles	4	1882	J. L. Banker to Charles Fernald
Deed	Fernald, Charles	4	1884	Thomas Bell to Charles Fernald (various)
Deed	Fernald, Charles	4	1885	Thomas Dibblee to Charles Fernald

Subject Hdgs./ Subdivision	Collection	Box	Date	Finder's Aid
REAL PROPERTY (cont.)				
Deed	Fernald, Charles	7	1886	Quit Claim Deed to half of Santa Rosa Island
Deed	Fernald, Charles	4	1888	Samuel Minor to Charles Fernald
Deed	Fernald, Charles	4	1888	Charles Fernald to Antonio & Leopoldo Schiappapietra
Deed	Fernald, Charles	5	1888	Charles Fernald to Thomas Bard (various)
Deed	Fernald, Charles	5	1888	Charles Fernald to Gordon Blanding
Deed	Fernald, Charles	4	1889	S. W. Backus to George W. Coffin (various)
Deed	Fernald, Charles	4	1889	James Wheeler to Charles Fernald (various)
Deed	Fernald, Charles	2	1875-89	Thomas Bard to Fernald & Richards (various)
Deed	Fernald, Charles	3	1876	Henry M. Newhall to Charles Fernald (various)
Deed	Fernald, Charles	4	1890	L. C. McKeeby to Charles Fernald
Deed	Fernald, Charles	2	1892	Thomas Bard to Fernald
Deed	Fernald, Charles	4	1884	Thomas Bell to Charles Fernald
Deed	Fernald, Charles	2	1879	Jose Lobero to Thomas Bard: Rancho Rio Santa Clara
Deed	Graves, Jackson A.	2	1894	Chino Valley Beet Sugar Co to H. W. O'Melveny
Deed	Graves, Jackson A.	3	1895	Carlos Olvera to H. W. O'Melveny
Deed	Graves, Jackson A.	79-80	1879	J. A. Graves to C. S. Andrews

Subject Hdgs./ Subdivision	*Collection*	*Box*	*Date*	*Finder's Aid*
REAL PROPERTY (cont.)				
Deed	Graves, Jackson A.	10	1901	Balfour, Guthrie & Co to Graves, O'Melveny and Shankland
Deed	Graves, Jackson A.	81-83	1882	Graves to J. A. Kelly
Deed	Graves, Jackson A.	9	1900	A. F. Morrison to Henry O'Melveny
Deed	Graves, Jackson A.	8	1899	Victor Montgomery to Henry W. O'Melveny
Deed	Graves, Jackson A.	81-83	1881	Graves & Chapman to J. M. Griffith
Deed	Graves, Jackson A.	1	1893	Sam M. Hyneman to Graves, O'Melveny & Shankland
Deed	Graves, Jackson A.	10	1901	Works & Lee to Graves, O'Melveny & Shankland
Deed	Graves, Jackson A.	3	1894	Stephen M. White to J. A. Graves
Deed	Graves, Jackson A.	2	1894	Carlos Olvera to H. W. O'Melveny
Deed	Graves, Jackson A.	4	1895	Frank B. Sturge to Henry O'Melveny
Deed	Halleck, Peachy, Billings	2	1854	Jose Pico to John Wilson of Rancho Piedra Blanca
Deed	Heslop Family	1	1885	Leander Dennis to C. C. Cook of Los Angeles land
Deed	Heslop Family	1	1893	Rancho Muscupiabe
Deed	Heslop Family	1	1887-97	Various land papers
Deed	Hoadley, Milo	1	1869	James Hoadley to Milo & Sarah Hoadley in San Francisco
Deed	Howell, E. L. W.	1	1870	Grant Deeds; form deeds for law firm of Mullan & Hyde; bargain & sale, quitclaims
Deed	Howell, Evelyn L. V.	1	1860-77	Warranty deed

Subject Hdgs./ Subdivision	Collection	Box	Date	Finder's Aid
REAL PROPERTY (cont.)				
Deed	Howell, Evelyn L. V.	1	1866-83	Various in Howell Land Papers
Deed	Jacks, David	C(5)	1884	S. O. Houghton to David Jacks
Deed	Jacks, David	C(4)	1883	S. O. Houghton to Jacks
Deed	Jacks, David	C(2)	1873	M. C. Ireland to David Jacks
Deed	Jacks, David	C(3)	1872	John Markley to David Jacks
Deed	Jacks, David	B(V-13)	1890	Deed: Jacks to F. Botsch
Deed	Jacks, David	C(2)	1873	F. M. Jolly to David Jacks
Deed	Keller, Matthew	2	1854-72	Los Angeles City Council to Keller
Deed	Keller, Matthew	3	1874	Handwritten Deed
Deed	Keller, Matthew	3	1877	Warranty Deed, Bargain & Sale Deed
Deed	Keller, Matthew	1	1868	Enrique Avila to Thomas Alvarado in Rancho Tajauta
Deed	Keller, Matthew	1	1869	Enrique Avila to Keller, Matthew in Rancho Tajauta
Deed	Keller, Matthew	1	1868	Juan Avila to Enrique Avila in Rancho Tajauta
Deed	Keller, Matthew	1	1861	Phineas Banning & Augustus Hinchman to Keller, Matthew in Wilmington
Deed	Keller, Matthew	1	1887	Menzo Boyce to Charles VanEvery in Santa Monica
Deed	Keller, Matthew	1	1872-81	James Burns to Various
Deed	Keller, Matthew	1	1872	Ozro Childs to Keller, Matthew in Rancho Nogales & Tajauta
Deed	Keller, Matthew	1	1877	Orzo Childs, etc. to J. Relihan in Mauuel Abril Tract in L. A.

Subject Hdgs./ Subdivision	*Collection*	*Box*	*Date*	*Finder's Aid*
REAL PROPERTY (cont.)				
Deed	Keller, Matthew	1	1864	John Downey to Keller, Matthew in Wilmington
Deed	Keller, Matthew	1	1869	John Downey to Keller, Matthew in Los Angeles
Deed	Keller, Matthew	1	1870	Gonzalez & Gonzalez to Keller, Matthew in San Gabriel Canyon
Deed	Keller, Matthew	1	1868-72	George Hanson to Keller of Various L. A. Properties
Deed	Keller, Matthew	1	1855	Hartman & Hartman to Keller, Matthew in L. A.
Deed	Keller, Matthew	2	1904	Caroline Leahy to Henry Keller in Santa Monica
Deed	Keller, Matthew	2	1854-73	Various deeds to Keller, Matthew from City of L. A. & L. A. Canal, Canal & Reservoir Co.
Deed	Keller, Matthew	3	1859	Lorenza Machado to Keller, Matthew in L. A.
Deed	Keller, Matthew	3	1895	Merlinjones & Merlinjones to Henry Keller in Santa Monica
Deed	Keller, Matthew	3	1864	William Moore to Keller, Matthew
Deed	Keller, Matthew	3	1856	Pio Pico to Keller, Matthew in Los Angeles
Deed	Keller, Matthew	3	1855	Ramirez & Ramirez to Isaac Harmtna in L. A.
Deed	Keller, Matthew	3	1856	Rimpau & Rimpau to Keller, Matthew in Los Angeles
Deed	Keller, Matthew	3	1875	Domenico Rivera to Keller, Matthew in Los Angeles

Subject Hdgs./ Subdivision	*Collection*	*Box*	*Date*	*Finder's Aid*
REAL PROPERTY (cont.)				
Deed	Keller, Matthew	3	1867	William Stanford to Keller, Matthew in L. A.
Deed	Keller, Matthew	3	1868	Jose Serrano to Enrique Avial of Rancho Tajauta
Deed	Keller, Matthew	3	1868	William Sex & James Holmes to Keller, Matthew in Rancho la Cienega (oil properties)
Deed	Keller, Matthew	3	1891	John Steer to Henry Keller in Santa Monica
Deed	Keller, Matthew	3	1875	George Tiffany to Keller, Matthew in L. A.
Deed	Keller, Matthew	3	1873	James Toberman to George Tiffany in L. A.
Deed	Keller, Matthew	3	1891	VanEvery & VanEvery to Henry Keller in Santa Monica
Deed	Keller, Matthew	3	1854	Horace Wheeler to Pio Pico in L. A.
Deed	Keller, Matthew	3	1892	Workman & Workman to Henry Keller in L. A.
Deed	Keller, Matthew	3	1897	Workman & Workman to Henry Keller in L. A. Workman Park Tract
Deed	Leidesdorff, William A.	1	1840-42	Land Grant: San Antonio Abad
Deed	Leidesdorff, William A.	5	1848	Leidesdorff & James Lick
Deed	Markham, H. H.	10	1890	Frank P. Kelly to H. H. Markham
Deed	Markham, H. H.	21	1875-93	H. H. Markham (various)
Deed	Markham, H. H.	1	1887	Died Bahten to H. H. Markham
Deed	Markham, H. H.	21	1898	Charles Olsen to H. H. Markham

Subject Hdgs./ Subdivision	*Collection*	*Box*	*Date*	*Finder's Aid*
REAL PROPERTY (cont.)				
Deed	Markham, H. H.	21	1883	D. R. Dickey to C. H. Walts, Etc.
Deed	Markham, H. H.	13	1896	Murphey & Gottschalk to H. H. Markham
Deed	Markham, H. H.	4	1895	John S. Chapman to H. H. Markham
Deed	New Almaden Mine	1	1861	Robert Cullen to Samuel Buttersworth, et al. Deed to land in Rancho de los Capitancillos, Santa Clara Co.
Deed	New Almaden Mine	1	1860	Robert Walker to Robert Cullen, deed to portion of Rancho de los Capitancillos, Santa Clara Co.
Deed	O'Farrell, Jasper	1	1851-55	Jasper O'Farrell to John O'Farrell
Deed	Potter, Charles & Isaac	1	1915	Cain irrigation Co. (various)
Deed	Potter, Charles & Isaac	3	1911	Hillside Water Co. & Nevada-Calif. Power Co.
Deed	Potter, Charles & Isaac	3	1922	Hydro-Electric Co.
Deed	Potter, Charles & Isaac	4	1920	Mono Power Company (various)
Deed	Potter, Charles & Isaac	5	1922-24	The Sierras Construction Co. (various)
Deed	Potter, Charles & Isaac	6	1918	The Southern Sierras Power Co. (various)
Deed	Potter, Charles & Isaac	7	1906	J. M. Elliott, et al. to Bd. of Water Com'rs of L. A. County
Deed	Potter, Charles & Isaac	7	1923	Southern Sierra Power Co. (various)

Subject Hdgs./ Subdivision	*Collection*	*Box*	*Date*	*Finder's Aid*
REAL PROPERTY (cont.)				
Deed	Shorb, James de Barth	20	1889	Chapman to Hendrick to James de Barth Shorb
Deed	Shorb, James de Barth	125	1890	Edward L. Watkins to George Smith Patton
Deed	Stimson, Marshall	10	1912-41	Various
Deed	Wolfskill, Lewis	1	1836	Edwardo Hernandez to William Wolfskill of lot in Los Angeles
Deed	Wolfskill, Lewis	1	1840	Expediente for lot in Los Angeles to Juan Dominguez
Deed	Wolfskill, Lewis	1	1842	Land Grant: Fernando Arguello to Maria de Ruiz of Los Angeles Land
Deed	Wolfskill, Lewis	1	1848	Charles White & Ellen White to Miles Goodyear of 50 acres in Santa Clara County
Deed	Wolfskill, Lewis	1	1849	William Wolfskill to John Wolfskill in Solano County
Deed	Wolfskill, Lewis	1	1852	Vallejo & Vallejo to Goodyear & Robinson in Rancho Suscol
Deed	Wolfskill, Lewis	1	1862	Domonguez to Alexander in Rancho San Pedro
Deed	Wolfskill, Lewis	1	1863	Francisco Correa to Manuel Romero in Los Angeles
Deed	Wolfskill, Lewis	1	1863	Alexander & Alexander to Dominguez in Rancho San Pedro
Deed	Wolfskill, Lewis	1	1866	Henry Dalton to Francis Pioche in Ranchos Azusa, San Jose, San Francisquito, & San Jose add.

Subject Hdgs./ Subdivision	Collection	Box	Date	Finder's Aid
REAL PROPERTY (cont.)				
Deed	Wolfskill, Lewis	2	1868	Henry Mellus to Eugene Meyer in San Gabriel
Deed	Wolfskill, Lewis	2	1869	Felipe Lastra to Lewis Wolfskill of La Asta Bandera mine in Inyo (var. other mines in Inyo Co.)
Deed	Wolfskill, Lewis	2	1870	Ralph Leon to Juan Lelong in L. A.
Deed	Wolfskill, Lewis	2	1871	William Spurgeon to Kenneth McKenzie in Los Angeles
Deed	Wolfskill, Lewis	2	1871	Dolores Sepulveda to Andrew Smith in Ranchos San Rafael & La Canada
Deed	Wolfskill, Lewis	2	1872	Kenneth McKenzie to Lewis Wolfskill in Los Angeles
Deed	Wolfskill, Lewis	2	1872	Pablo Laughlin to Lewis Wolfskill in Los Angeles
Deed	Wolfskill, Lewis	3	1873	Various acquired by Lewis Wolfskill in Los Angeles
Deed	Wolfskill, Lewis	4	1874	Various to Lewis Wolfskill incl. tax sale deeds
Deed	Wolfskill, Lewis	5	1875	Various to Lewis Wolfskill and Wolfskill to various
Deed	Wolfskill, Lewis	6	1876-77	Various to Wolfskill
Deed	Wolfskill, Lewis	6	1877	Henry Dalton to Lewis Wolfskill in Ranchos Azusa, San Jose Add., and San Jose
Deed	Wolfskill, Lewis	7	1877-78	Various to Wolfskill

Subject Hdgs./ Subdivision	*Collection*	*Box*	*Date*	*Finder's Aid*
REAL PROPERTY (cont.)				
Deed	Wolfskill, Lewis	7	1877	Francisco Lopez to John D. Bicknell in Los Angeles
Deed	Wolfskill, Lewis	8	1878	Maria Navarro to Lewis Wolfskill
Deed	Wolter, Charles	1	1848	Deed - Jose M. Escobar to Encainacion Garcia
Deed	Wolter, Charles	2	1855	Quitclaim form
Deed	Wolter, Charles	2	1856	Quitclaim form
Ejectment	Fernald, Charles	3	1877	Leo Juston to Charles Fernald
Eminent Domain	Fernald, Charles	3	1877	J. D. Patterson to Charles Fernald
Eminent Domain	Graves, Jackson A.	4	1896	Charles P. Eels to H. W. O'Melveny
Eminent Domain	Potter, Chas & Tsaac	4	1920	Mono Power Company (various)
Eminent Domain	Wolfskill, Lewis	5	1875	Notice of Condemnation
	Jacks, David	BII3	1888	Account of Ingvard Lund to Jacks
	Jacks, David	BV14	1864	Jacks to Thomas Allen
Mining	Morgan, William Rollin	1	1872-73	William Morgan to Mina Morgan (various)
Mortgage	Aram, Joseph	1	1895	Joseph Aram to Eugene Aram
Mortgage	Baker, Robert	2	1878	John Wise to Robert Baker
Mortgage	Baldwin, Anita M.	5	1898	Lovell White to H. A. Unruh
Mortgage	Baldwin, Anita M.	5	1898	H. A. Unruh to Lovell White
Mortgage	Barclay, Henry	3	1905	Taylor, Elizah to Edgar W. Barrett, Rancho San Rafael
Mortgage	Barclay, Henry	4	1893	Muscupiabe Rancho, Barclay M.
Mortgage	Barclay, Henry	1	1897	Fox, et al. vs. Irvington Land & Water Co.

Subject Hdgs./ Subdivision	*Collection*	*Box*	*Date*	*Finder's Aid*
REAL PROPERTY (cont.)				
Mortgage	Center, John	1	1858	John Center to Quartus Sparks on San Francisco Lot
Mortgage	Center, John	3	1861	John Center to Moses Ellis
Mortgage	Center, John	6	1863	John Center to Frances Fleming
Mortgage	Crank, James F.	3	1887-91	James Crank to various in 3 Letterbooks
Mortgage	Fernald, Charles	2	1875-89	Thomas Bard to Fernald & Richards (various)
Mortgage	Fernald, Charles	3	1876	Henry M. Newhall to Charles Fernald (various)
Mortgage	Fernald, Charles	4	1890	L. C. McKeeby to Charles Fernald
Mortgage	Fernald, Charles	3	1876	Lovell White to Wallace More
Mortgage	Fernald, Charles	3	1876	E. A. Edwards to Charles Fernald
Mortgage	Fernald, Charles	3	1876	Joseph Perkins to Charles Fernald
Mortgage	Fernald, Charles	4	1880	R. S. Brooks to Charles Fernald
Mortgage	Fernald, Charles	4	1880	Lancaster Ould to Charles Fernald (various)
Mortgage	Fernald, Charles	4	1880	R. Steinback to Charles Fernald
Mortgage	Fernald, Charles	4	1881	Thomas Bell to Charles Fernald (various)
Mortgage	Fernald, Charles	4	1881	A. D. Moore to Charles Fernald
Mortgage	Fernald, Charles	4	1881	A. Packard to Charles Fernald (various)
Mortgage	Fernald, Charles	4	1881	Theodore Wetzel to Charles Fernald
Mortgage	Fernald, Charles	4	1885	W. Mayo Newhall to Charles Fernald
Mortgage	Fernald, Charles	4	1887	Edward J. Pringle to Charles Fernald
Mortgage	Fernald, Charles	4	1887	William Cowles to Charles Fernald
Mortgage	Fernald, Charles	7	1880	Henry C. McPike to Charles Fernald

Subject Hdgs./ Subdivision	Collection	Box	Date	Finder's Aid
REAL PROPERTY (cont.)				
Mortgage	Fernald, Charles	3	1876	A. W. Thompason to Charles Fernald
Mortgage	Fernald, Charles	3	1878	William C. Howard to Charles Fernald
Mortgage	Fernald, Charles	3	1878	Lancaster Ould to Charles Fernald (various)
Mortgage	Fernald, Charles	4	1879	E. A. Heacock to Charles Fernald
Mortgage	Fernald, Charles	4	1879	Lancaster Ould to Charles Fernald (various)
Mortgage	Fernald, Charles	4	1885	Henry Newhall to Charles Fernald (various)
Mortgage	Fernald, Charles	4	1886	Henry Newhall to Charles Fernald (various)
Mortgage	Fernald, Charles	4	1880	Lovell White to Charles Fernald
Mortgage	Fernald, Charles	4	1881	R. Steinbach to Charles Fernald
Mortgage	Fernald, Charles	4	1885	Rudolph Steinbach to Charles Fernald
Mortgage	Fernald, Charles	4	1885	George C. Perkins to Charles Fernald (various)
Mortgage	Fernald, Charles	4	1886	George C. Perkins to Charles Fernald
Mortgage	Graves, Jackson A.	9	1900	J. Jones to J. A. Graves
Mortgage	Graves, Jackson A.	10	1901	T. J. Smith to Dear Sirs (Graves, O'Melveny & Shankland)
Mortgage	Graves, Jackson A.	11	1914	Jackson A. Graves to I. W. Hellman
Mortgage	Graves, Jackson A.	11	1915	Jackson A. Graves to I. W. Hellman
Mortgage	Graves, Jackson A.	10	1901	American Surety Co. to Graves, O'Melveny & Shankland
Mortgage	Graves, Jackson A.	10	1901	D. A. Moore to Dear Sir (Graves)

Subject Hdgs./ Subdivision	Collection	Box	Date	Finder's Aid
REAL PROPERTY (cont.)				
Mortgage	Graves, Jackson A.	8	1899	William Rose to Graves, O'Melveny and Shankland
Mortgage	Graves, Jackson A.	8	1899	Ventura Abstract Co. to J. A. Graves
Mortgage	Graves, Jackson A.	8	1900	Consolidated Abstract & Title Guarantee Co. to Graves, O'Melveny & Shankland
Mortgage	Graves, Jackson A.	8	1899	Isaias Hellman to J. A. Graves
Mortgage	Graves, Jackson A.	8	1899	Balfour, Guthrie & Co. to Graves, O'Melveny & Shankland
Mortgage	Graves, Jackson A.	1	1892	Various to Graves, O'Melveny & Shankland
Mortgage	Graves, Jackson A.	1	1892	Reinstein & Eisner to J. A. Graves
Mortgage	Graves, Jackson A.	1	1892	J. F. Satori to Graves, O'Melveny & Shankland (various)
Mortgage	Graves, Jackson A.	1	1893	Balfour, Guthrie & Co. to Graves, O'Melveny & Shankland (various)
Mortgage	Graves, Jackson A.	1	1893	C. G. Brown to J. A. Graves
Mortgage	Graves, Jackson A.	1	1893	Curtis, Oster & Curtis to Graves, O'Melveny & Shankland
Mortgage	Graves, Jackson A.	3	1895	E. J. LeBretou to J. A. Graves
Mortgage	Graves, Jackson A.	3	1895	H. Hawes to H. W. O'Melveny
Mortgage	Graves, Jackson A.	3	1895	Isaias Hellman to J. A. Graves

Subject Hdgs./ Subdivision	Collection	Box	Date	Finder's Aid
REAL PROPERTY (cont.)				
Mortgage	Graves, Jackson A.	2	1894	C. J. Brown to J. A. Graves
Mortgage	Graves, Jackson A.	2	1894	Curtis, Oster & Curtis to J. A. Graves, H. W. O'Melveny & J. H. Shankland (various)
Mortgage	Graves, Jackson A.	2	1894	Arthur Hutchinson to Henry W. O'Melveny
Mortgage	Graves, Jackson A.	2	1894	A. S. Kimball to J. A. Graves
Mortgage	Graves, Jackson A.	2	1894	W. J. McIntyre to H. W. O'Melveny
Mortgage	Graves, Jackson A.	5	1897	Fabius O. Daniel to J. A. Graves, H. W. O'Melveny & J. H. Shankland
Mortgage	Graves, Jackson A.	7	1898	Title Insurance & Trust Co. to J. A. Graves, H. W. O'Melveny & J. H. Shankland
Mortgage	Graves, Jackson A.	11	1920	Jackson A. Graves to E. S. Heller and Sidney M. Ehrman
Mortgage	Graves, Jackson A.	9	1900	Isaias Hellman to H. W. O'Melveny
Mortgage	Graves, Jackson A.	8	1900	William Collins to Graves, O'Melveny and Shankland
Mortgage	Graves, Jackson A.	8	1899	E. W. Hendrick to J. A. Graves
Mortgage	Graves, Jackson A.	8	1899	Robert Slaughter to H. W. O'Melveny
Mortgage	Graves, Jackson A.	1	1892	Balfour, Guthrie & Co. to Graves, O'Melveny & Shankland
Mortgage	Graves, Jackson A.	2	1893	W. M. Caswell to Graves, O'Melveny & Shankland
Mortgage	Graves, Jackson A.	2	1894	Isaias Hellman to J. A. Graves

Subject Hdgs./ Subdivision	*Collection*	*Box*	*Date*	*Finder's Aid*
REAL PROPERTY (cont.)				
Mortgage	Graves, Jackson A.	5	1897	Balfour, Guthrie to J. A. Graves, H. W. O'Melveny & J. H. Shankland (various)
Mortgage	Graves, Jackson A.	5	1897	Charles Bishop to J. A. Graves, H. W. O'Melveny & J. H. Shankland
Mortgage	Graves, Jackson A.	5	1897	French Savings Bank to J. Graves
Mortgage	Graves, Jackson A.	5	1897	R. B. Huston to Henry O'Melveny
Mortgage	Graves, Jackson A.	88-90	1890	Graves, O'Melveny & Shankland to Jarboe, Harrison & Goodfellow
Mortgage	Graves, Jackson A.	9	1900	John G. North to H. W. O'Melveny
Mortgage	Graves, Jackson A.	2	1893	George Porter to J. A. Graves
Mortgage	Graves, Jackson A.	4	1896	Edward Annable to J. A. Graves, H. W. O'Melveny & J. H. Shankland
Mortgage	Graves, Jackson A.	2	1894	Isaias Hellman to J. A. Graves
Mortgage	Haight, Henry	5	1860	Henry Haight & Savings & Loan Society
Mortgage	Heslop Family	1	1894-97	Rancho Santa Anita
Mortgage	Hoadley, Milo	1	1881	Hoadley & Santa Cruz Bank
Mortgage	Howell, Evelyn L. V.	1	1875-90	Various in Howell Land Papers
Mortgage	Jacks, David	C5	1885	S. O. Houghton to David Jacks
Mortgage	Keller, Matthew	2	1870	Keller, Matthew to Antoine Borel
Mortgage	Keller, Matthew	2	1872	Various to Francois Gasne
Mortgage	Keller, Matthew	1	1879	Antoine Borel to Keller, Matthew
Mortgage	Markham, H. H.	15	1896	George E. Pratt to H. H. Markham

Subject Hdgs./ Subdivision	*Collection*	*Box*	*Date*	*Finder's Aid*
REAL PROPERTY (cont.)				
Mortgage	Markham, H. H.	4	1885	James M. Craig to H. H. Markham
Mortgage	Markham, H. H.	6	1890	R. J. Floyd to H. H. Markham
Mortgage	Markham, H. H.	14	1885	J. M. Obando to H. H. Markham
Mortgage	Markham, H. H.	19	1882	J. B. Whitfield to H. H. Markham
Mortgage	Markham, H. H.	12	1896	Richard J. Mason to H. H. Markham
Mortgage	Markham, H. H.	18	1896	James F. Towell to H. H. Markham
Mortgage	Markham, H. H.	11	1897	Peter McVicar to H. H. Markham
Mortgage	Markham, H. H.	2	1890	John D. Bicknell to H. H. Markham
Mortgage	Markham, H. H.	3	1897	J. F. Campbell to H. H. Markham
Mortgage	Morgan, William Rollin	2	1881	Samuel Kingdom to William Morgan
Mortgage	Morgan, William Rollin	2	1882	Daniel Titus to William Morgan
Mortgage	Morgan, William Rollin	2	1886	James Jones to H. H. Thomas
Mortgage	Morgan, William Rollin	2	1888	Time Donaghue to William Morgan
Mortgage	Potter, Charles & Isaac	1	1915-33	Cain Irrigation Co. (various)
Mortgage	Potter, Charles & Isaac	1	1915	Cain Irrigation Co. to Anglo-Calif. Trust Co. (various)
Mortgage	Potter, Charles & Isaac	4	1916	Nevada-Calif. Power Co. (various)
Mortgage	Potter, Charles & Isaac	5	1916	Nevada-Calif. Electric Corp. (various)
Mortgage	Potter, Charles & Isaac	5	1910	Pacific Power Co. (various)
Mortgage	Potter, Charles & Isaac	6	1918	The Southern Sierras Power Co. (various)

Subject Hdgs./ Subdivision	*Collection*	*Box*	*Date*	*Finder's Aid*
REAL PROPERTY (cont.)				
Mortgage	Potter, Charles & Isaac	6	1917	Corona Gas & Electric Light Co. (various)
Mortgage	Potter, Charles & Isaac	7	1923	Southern Sierra Power Co. (various)
Mortgage	Shorb, James de Barth	2	1893	James M. Allen to E. T. Wright
Mortgage	Shorb, James de Barth	7	1889	Balfour, Guthrie & Co. to James de Barth Shorb
Mortgage	Shorb, James de Barth	97	1899	Chris Randolph to Maria Shorb
Mortgage	Shorb, James de Barth	199	1886-93	San Francisco Savings Union to James de Barth Shorb (various)
Mortgage	Shorb, James de Barth	81	1886	Francis Newlands to James de Barth Shorb
Mortgage	Shorb, James de Barth	103	1899	James Shankland to Maria Shorb
Mortgage	Shorb, James de Barth	103	1899	James Shankland to Maria Shorb
Mortgage	Shorb, James de Barth	20	1891-92	M. R. Chew to James M. Tiernan (various)
Mortgage	Stimson, Marshall	10	1912-41	Various
Mortgage	Terry, David Smith	3	1870	G. W. Graham to David Terry
Mortgage	Terry, David Smith	3	1870	David Terry to Cornelia Terry
Mortgage	Wolfskill, Lewis	2	1869	Henry Dalton to Francis Pioche
Mortgage	Wolfskill, Lewis	5	1875	James M. Taylor to Lewis Wolfskill (Rancho San Francisquito litigation)
Mortgage	Wolfskill, Lewis	5	1875	Henry Dalton to Lewis Wolfskill Rancho Azusa
Mortgage	Wolfskill, Lewis	6	1876	Magee & Magee to Meyer in L. A.
Mortgage	Wolfskill, Lewis	6	1876	Dalton & Dalton to Wolfskill on Rancho Azusa Homestead

Subject Hdgs./ Subdivision	***Collection***	***Box***	***Date***	***Finder's Aid***
REAL PROPERTY (cont.)				
Mortgage	Potter, Charles & Isaac	1	1915-24	Cain Irrigation Co. to Anglo-Calif. Trust Co. (various)
Oil	Fernald, Charles	2	1892	Thomas Bard to Fernald
	Shorb, James de Barth	116	1888	William Morris Stewart to James de Barth Shorb
	Fernald, Charles	4	1888	J. M. Fillmore to Charles Fernald (various)
Reconveyance	Graves, Jackson A.	10	1901	Balfour, Guthrie & Co. to Graves, O'Melveny and Shankland
Recording	Jacks, David	C(3)	1872	John Markley to David Jacks
Redemption	Fernald, Charles	4	1882	Charles Fernald to E. B. Hall (various)
Redemption	Fernald, Charles	4	1881	D. L. Dow to Charles Fernald
Rescission	Fernald, Charles	2	1879	Jose Lobero to Thomas Bard: Rancho Rio Santa Clara
Sales	Keller, Matthew	2	1854-72	Los Angeles City Council to Keller
Sales	Jacks, David	BV10	1873	Bill of Sale of Joseph Johnson
Tax Titles	Fernald, Charles	3	1876	Wilson & Wilson to Charles Fernald (various)
Tax Titles	Graves, Jackson A.	81-83	1882	Graves to J. A. Kelly
Tax Titles	Graves, Jackson A.	85-86	1886	Graves, O'Melveny to W. J. Smith
Taxation	Fernald, Charles	4	1888	J. M. Fillmore to Charles Fernald (various)
Taxation	Graves, Jackson A.	3	1895	J. A. Graves to S. B. Pierce
Title	Azusa-Foothill Cit.	1	1844-80	Hudson, Gillette & Gibson Abstract, Rancho Azusa
Title	Azusa-Foothill Cit.	1	1886	Houghton, Silent & Campbell abstract, Azusa Rancho

Subject Hdgs./ Subdivision	Collection	Box	Date	Finder's Aid
REAL PROPERTY (cont.)				
Title	Baker, Robert	4	1879	Charles Forbes to Baker, Robert
Title	Baker, Robert	2	1878	Charles Forbes to Baker, Robert
Title	Barclay, Henry	1	1887-08	Pioneer Abstract and Title Guarantee Co. (various)
Title	Barclay, Henry	3	1894	Tujunga Rancho, L. A. Co.
Title	Barclay, Henry	3	1868-87	Helen A. M. Morris, Rancho San Bernardino
Title	Barclay, Henry	3	1889	Title Opinion Barclay, Wilson & Carpenter: Tujunga Rancho
Title	Barclay, Henry	3	1901	Margaret R. MacLeod, Tujunga Rancho
Title	Barclay, Henry	4	1872	Rancho Muscupiabe
Title	Barclay, Henry	4	1885-05	Abstract, Muscupiabc Rancho Deeds (various)
Title	Barclay, Henry	4	1886	Barclay & Wilson vs. Akers, et al. to quiet title
Title	Barclay, Henry	4	1889	Barclay, Wilson & Carpenter Title Opinion, Rancho Muscupiabe
Title	Barclay, Henry	4	1899	Barclay, H. A. to F. H. Brigham
Title	Barclay, Henry	4	1909	Munson & Barclay to B. F. Bledove Rancho Muscupiabe: points & authorities in Superior Court
Title	Brent, Joseph	3	1869	Wilson, Ben. J. to Joseph Brent
Title	Brent, Joseph	3	1878	Sepulveda, Ignacio to Joseph Brent
Title	Brent, Joseph	3	1870	Downey, John G. to Joseph Brent
Title	Catlin, Amos P.	1	1853	F. S. Mumford to Catlin

Subject Hdgs./ Subdivision	*Collection*	*Box*	*Date*	*Finder's Aid*
REAL PROPERTY (cont.)				
Title	Center, John	1	1855	William Walton to John Center
Title	Center, John	4	1863	Various statements of intent to claim tracts of land
Title	Center, John	5	1867	P. Van Trump to Samuel Crim
Title	Chipman-Dwinelle	1	1879	Abstract of Alameda Lots
Title	Chipman-Dwinelle	3	1879	Abstract of Alameda Lot
Title	Chipman-Dwinelle	5	1880	Abstract, Encinal Park Tract, Alameda
Title	Chipman-Dwinelle	Folder 1	1855-19	Encinal San Antonio Papers
Title	Chipman-Dwinelle	1	1867	Comments of C.E.P. on Public Lands Decisions
Title	Chipman-Dwinelle	1		Sale of home; Transfer of Title
Title	Crank, James F.	11	1862-88	Abstract of Rancho San Pascual and Santa Anita
Title	Fernald, Charles	3	1860	Charles Huse to Charles Fernald
Title	Fernald, Charles	3	1876	Smith and Redington to Charles Fernald (various)
Title	Fernald, Charles	4	1879	Bledsoe & McKeeby to Charles Fernald
Title	Fernald, Charles	4	1880	S. Bristol to Charles Fernald
Title	Fernald, Charles	4	1890	Paul R. Wright to Samuel Backus
Title	Fernald, Charles	4	1890	Herbert Fryer to Charles Fernald
Title	Fernald, Charles	5	1886	Charles Fernald to H. W. Moore
Title	Fernald, Charles	1	1889-90	Bell vs. Foxen Litigation Papers, Rancho Laguna de San Francisco
Title	Fernald, Charles	6	1887	Williams vs. Hart case file

Subject Hdgs./ Subdivision	Collection	Box	Date	Finder's Aid
REAL PROPERTY (cont.)				
Title	Fernald, Charles	8	1861-64	Various, Rancho Calleguas
Title	Fernald, Charles	8	1874	Abstract of Title of Rancho La Goleta
Title	Fernald, Charles	8	1875	Rancho San Francisco
Title	Fernald, Charles	8	1864	Rancho San Pedro
Title	Fernald, Charles	8	1869	Rancho Santa Anita
Title	Fernald, Charles	8	1852-89	Various abstracts and documents, City of Santa Barbara
Title	Fernald, Charles	8	1872	U. S. Patent, City of Santa Barbara
Title	Fernald, Charles	8	1890	Charles Fernald to Antonio Schiappapietra
Title	Fernald, Charles	3	1858	W. R. P. Washburn to Charles Fernald
Title	Fernald, Charles	4	1889	James Wheeler to Charles Fernald (various)
Title	Fernald, Charles	3	1876	Thomas A. Scott to Charles Fernald
Title	Graves, Jackson A.	9	1900	A. F. Morrison to Henry O'Melveny
Title	Graves, Jackson A.	8	1899	Victor Montgomery to Henry O'Melveny
Title	Graves, Jackson A.	81-83	1881	Graves & Chapman to J. M. Griffith
Title	Graves, Jackson A.	11	1918	Jackson A. Graves to I. W. Hellman
Title	Graves, Jackson A.	11	1924	Jackson A. Graves to E. S. Pillsbury
Title	Graves, Jackson A.	10	1900	Binger Herman to Register & Receiver
Title	Graves, Jackson A.	10	1901	D. A. Chambers to H. W. O'Melveny
Title	Graves, Jackson A.	8	1900	D. A. Chambers to H. W. O'Melveny
Title	Graves, Jackson A.	1	1891	F. A. Hyde to W. J. Curtis

Subject Hdgs./ Subdivision	*Collection*	*Box*	*Date*	*Finder's Aid*
REAL PROPERTY (cont.)				
Title	Graves, Jackson A.	1	1891	M. L. Wocks to Jackson Graves (various)
Title	Graves, Jackson A.	1	1892	D. F. Rillinghast to Graves, O'Melveny & Shankland (various)
Title	Graves, Jackson A.	1	1892	James F. Peck to H. W. O'Melveny
Title	Graves, Jackson A.	1	1892	Robinson & Patterson to Graves, O'Melveny & Shankland
Title	Graves, Jackson A.	1	1893	Various to Graves
Title	Graves, Jackson A.	1	1893	Courtney Clarke to Graves, O'Melveny & Shankland
Title	Graves, Jackson A.	1	1893	W. P. Gardiner to Henry O'Melveny
Title	Graves, Jackson A.	1	1893	James M. Gully to J. A. Graves
Title	Graves, Jackson A.	1	1893	Arthur Hutchinson to Graves, O'Melveny & Shankland
Title	Graves, Jackson A.	2	1893	A. B. Manahan to H. W. O'Melveny
Title	Graves, Jackson A.	2	1893	William H. Pratt to Stephen M. White
Title	Graves, Jackson A.	3	1895	Luis Arques to H. W. O'Melveny
Title	Graves, Jackson A.	3	1894	L. P. Cannon to J. A. Graves, H. W. O'Melveny & J. H. Shankland
Title	Graves, Jackson A.	3	1894	Stephen M. White to J. A. Graves
Title	Graves, Jackson A.	2	1894	Carlos Olvera to H. W. O'Melveny
Title	Graves, Jackson A.	4	1896	A. J. Lightner to H. A. Graves
Title	Graves, Jackson A.	3	1895	W. S. Melick to J. A. Graves

Subject Hdgs./ Subdivision	*Collection*	*Box*	*Date*	*Finder's Aid*
REAL PROPERTY (cont.)				
Title	Graves, Jackson A.	4	1895	Title Insurance and Trust Co. to J. A. Graves, H. W. O'Melveny & J. H. Shankland
Title	Graves, Jackson A.	4	1895	Wick, Wicks & Macdonald to J. A. Graves, H. W. O'Melveny & J. H. Shankland
Title	Graves, Jackson A.	5	1897	Luis Arques to H. W. O'Melveny
Title	Graves, Jackson A.	5	1897	A. C. Blach to Henry O'Melveny
Title	Graves, Jackson A.	5	1897	Barnes & Selby to J. A. Graves, H. W. O'Melveny & J. H. Shankland
Title	Graves, Jackson A.	5	1897	D. A. Chambers to H. W. O'Melveny
Title	Graves, Jackson A.	5	1897	Consolidated Abstract & Title Guarantee Co. to J. A. Graves, H. W. O'Melveny & J. H. Shankland
Title	Graves, Jackson A.	7	1898	A. R. Metcalfe to H. W. Hellman
Title	Graves, Jackson A.	7	1898	William Singer, Jr. (Southern Pacific RR) to various
Title	Graves, Jackson A.	6	1898	J. A. Graves to A. Kortright Neales
Title	Graves, Jackson A.	6	1897	Carlos Olvera to H. W. O'Melveny
Title	Graves, Jackson A.	6	1897	Riverside Abstract Co. to J. A. Graves, H. W. O'Melveny & J. H. Shankland
Title	Graves, Jackson A.	88-90 LB	1880	Graves to Thomas Bell
Title	Graves, Jackson A.	3	1895	Henry O'Melveny to Buz (Jackson A. Graves)

Subject Hdgs./ Subdivision	Collection	Box	Date	Finder's Aid
REAL PROPERTY (cont.)				
Title	Graves, Jackson A.	79-80 LB	1880	Graves & Chapman to Shainwald Bros. report on Benson property in Pasadena
Title	Graves, Jackson A.	85-86 LB	1885	Henry O'Melveny to Miss Lester
Title	Graves, Jackson A.	88-89 LB	1889	Graves to friend J. B. Rheinstein
Title	Graves, Jackson A.	88-89 LB	1888	Graves, O'Melveny & Shankland to Rudolph Hopf
Title	Haight, Henry	1	1850	Henry Haight to Fletcher Haight
Title	Haight, Henry	2	1854	William L. Smith to Joseph Wells
Title	Haight, Henry	3	1854	William L. Smith to Joseph Wells
Title	Haight, Henry	3	1854	Fletcher M. Haight to Henry Haight
Title	Haight, Henry	3	1854	Joseph Gary to Henry Haight
Title	Haight, Henry	4	1856	Benjamin Orrick to Henry Haight
Title	Haight, Henry	4	1856	George Shurtleff to Henry Haight
Title	Haight, Henry	5	1858	John B. Wood Survey and Division along Petaluma Creek
Title	Haight, Henry	6	1869	Henry Haight to California Senators and Representa-tives in Congress
Title	Halleck, Peachy, Billings	1	1839-41	Transfer Deed to Rancho Jesus Maria; various documents
Title	Halleck, Peachy, Billings	1	1852-56	Various Land Claim Case materials
Title	Halleck, Peachy, Billings	1	1852	Brief; Land Claim Case #355
Title	Halleck, Peachy, Billings	2	1849-60	Various Land Claim Case materials

Subject Hdgs./ Subdivision	Collection	Box	Date	Finder's Aid
REAL PROPERTY (cont.)				
Title	Halleck, Peachy, Billings	2	1857	Brief, Mission San Luis Obispo
Title	Halleck, Peachy, Billings	2	1854	Pueblo of Santa Barbara
Title	Halleck, Peachy, Billings	2	1855-56	Santa Rosa Island claims case (various)
Title	Halleck, Peachy, Billings	2	1854	Rancho Simi claims case
Title	Halleck, Peachy, Billings	2	1854	Rancho Los Tularcitos claims case
Title	Halleck, Peachy, Billings	2	1858	Weber v. Woods (Rancho Campo de los Francises)
Title	Halleck, Peachy, Billings	2	1857	Stafford v. Lick
Title	Halleck, Peachy, Billings	2	1851	Marians Galvez to Eustguio Barron
Title	Halleck, Peachy, Billings	2	1855	Peachy's brief on "ten League" question
Title	Halleck, Peachy, Billings	1	1855	Testimony, Rancho Campo del los Franceses. Cal. Land Claims Case
Title	Halleck, Peachy, Billings	1	1853	Rancho Canada de los Capitanullos
Title	Halleck, Peachy, Billings	1	1852	Rancho Collayomi (various)
Title	Halleck, Peachy, Billings	1	1844	Expediente for Rancho Cosumnes
Title	Halleck, Peachy, Billings	1	1855-57	Rancho Guadalasca brief and proceedings, land claims case (various)
Title	Heslop Family	1	1833-35	Expediente of San Pascual Rancho
Title	Heslop Family	1	1858	Confirmation of title, San Pascual Rancho to Manuel Garfias
Title	Houghton, Shrmn O.	1	1885-88	Abstract of portion Rancho Azusa
Title	Jacks, David	C(5)	1886	John Bauman to Jacks
Title	Jacks, David	BV414	1880	Lease: Jacks to Manuel George

Subject Hdgs./ Subdivision	Collection	Box	Date	Finder's Aid
REAL PROPERTY (cont.)				
Title	Jacks, David	C(6)	1887	J. F. Birlem to Jacks
Title	Jacks, David	BV14	1870	Jacks to Buell
Title	Jacks, David	C6	1888	James A. Clayton to Jacks
Title	Jacks, David	BII3	1870	Samuel Casiday acct ledger to Jacks
Title	Jacks, David	BII3	1879	Sheep Account
Title	Jacks, David	C8	1890	Paul Talbot to Jacks
Title	Jacks, David	BII3	1879	Acc't. by W. H. Clark on Hamilton Property
Title	Keller, Matthew	1	1870	Glassell, Chapman & Smith Title Opinion on Keller L. A. Properties
Title	Keller, Matthew	1	1880	Abstract of L. A. Vineyard
Title	Leidesdorff, Wm. A.	6	1866	Archibald Peachy to J. L. Folsom
Title	Markham, H. H.	13	1896	Murphey & Gottschalk to H. H. Markham
Title	McCullough, S. L.B.	1	1858	Samuel McCullough to Caroline McCullough about Sacramento
Title	McCullough, S. L.B.	1	1870-71	Treat Tracts (S.F.) property owners. Minutes of meeting with attorneys
Title	Orange County Land Papers	1	1887-13	Various to Orange Co. Title Co.
Title	Orange County Land Papers	2	1885-15	Various to Orange Co. Title Co.
Title	Shorb, James de Barth	1	1909	H. O. Adams to George Smith Patton
Title	Shorb, James de Barth	14	1911	Thomas B. Brown to Maria de Jesus Wilson Shorb
Title	Shorb, James de Barth	45	1890	William W. Foote to James de Barth Shorb

Subject Hdgs./ Subdivision	*Collection*	*Box*	*Date*	*Finder's Aid*
REAL PROPERTY (cont.)				
Title	Shorb, James de Barth	105	1883	James de Barth Shorb to Creed Haymond
Title	Shorb, James de Barth	89	1887	Henry O'Melveny to James de Barth Shorb
Title	Stearns, Abel	4	1852-70	Jose M. Bandini correspondence
Title	Stearns, Abel	27	1852-69	Stephen Foster correspondence
Title	Stearns, Abel	27	1847-54	John C. Fremont correspondence
Title	Stearns, Abel	33	1846	Eliab Grimes correspondence
Title	Stearns, Abel	33	1858-59	Henry Halleck correspondence
Title	Stearns, Abel	34	1818-70	Samuel King correspondence
Title	Stearns, Abel	38	1853	Patrick Lambert correspondence
Title	Stearns, Abel	40	1845-46	Thomas Larkin correspondence
Title	Stearns, Abel	42	1833-62	James McKinley correspondence
Title	Stearns, Abel	46	1852	Isaac S. K. Ogier correspondence
Title	Stearns, Abel	46	1846-63	Jasper O'Farrell correspondence
Title	Stearns, Abel	46	1856	Pacific Ord correspondence
Title	Stearns, Abel	64	1853	Thomas Sutherland correspondence
Title	Stearns, Abel	66	1852-62	Joseph P. Thompson correspondence
Title	Stearns, Abel	67	1868	Lauren Upson correspondence
Title	Stearns, Abel	69	1854	James Wilson correspondence
Title	Wolfskill, Lewis		1869	Edmond Goold to Sherman Day, Claimants Brief, Rancho San Jose, Azusa & San Jose addition
Title	Wolfskill, Lewis	4	1874	Henry Dalton to John Brooks Felton

Subject Hdgs./ Subdivision	*Collection*	*Box*	*Date*	*Finder's Aid*
REAL PROPERTY (cont.)				
Title	Wolfskill, Lewis	5	1875	Henry Dalton to John Felton
Title	Wolfskill, Lewis	5	1875	Henry Dalton to Lewis Wolfskill
Title	Wolfskill, Lewis	6	1876	Abstract to L. A. lot
Title	Wolfskill, Lewis	8	1878	Notice of title, intent to evict
Title	Wolfskill, Lewis	8	1878	Abstract of L. A. lot
Title	Fernald, Charles	4	1883	H. C. Campbell to Charles Fernald
Title	Jacks, David	C(2)	1873	F. M. Jolly to David Jacks
Title	Wolter, Charles	2	1855	Quitclaim form
Title	Wolter, Charles	2	1856	Quitclaim form
Trespass	Markham, H. H.	18	1885	U. S. Land Office to D. J. Chadwick
Trespass	Shorb, James de Barth	110	1885	Bayard T. Smith to James M. Tiernan
Trespass	Fernald, Charles	3	1877	W. J. Graves to Charles Fernald
Trespass	Fernald, Charles	4	1887	Lazard Freres to Charles Fernald
Trespass	Graves, Jackson A.	7	1898	I. Jones to J. A. Graves, H. W. O'Melveny & J. H. Shankland
Trespass	Fernald, Charles	2	1894	I. Jones to J. A. Graves, H. W. O'Melveny & J. H. Shankland (various)
Trespass	Jacks, David	C(1)	1872	David Jacks to Juan Leon
Trespass	Jacks, David	C(2)	1873	David Jacks to Jr. R. Sheppard, Esq.
Trespass	Jacks, David	C(5)	1884	David Jacks to H. E. Abbott
Trespass	Jacks, David	C(2)	1874	J. M. Soto to David Jacks
Trust	Graves, Jackson A.	3	1894	S. D. Rosenbaum to J. A. Graves
Water	Shorb, James de Barth	9	1889	Y. Bayha to James de Barth Shorb
Water	Shorb, James de Barth	128	1891	Stephen M. White to James de Barth Shorb

Subject Hdgs./ Subdivision	*Collection*	*Box*	*Date*	*Finder's Aid*
REAL PROPERTY (cont.)				
Wine Business	Shorb, James de Barth	81	1887	National Viticulture Association to James de Barth Shorb
Wine Business	Shorb, James de Barth	116	1890	Charles Stern to James de Barth Shorb
TAXATION				
	Adams & Co.	4	1875	Moore v. Mark Hopkins
	Baker, Robert	2	1878	Gratton Perry to Baker, Robert
	Bowron, Fletcher	2	1946	"Conditions Which Led to Adoption of New Revenue Measures in L. A."
	Bowron, Fletcher	33	1939	Address: "Fed. Gov't. Taxation"
	Bowron, Fletcher	33	1940	"Statement... Feb. 1, 1940"
	Bowron, Fletcher	42	1961	"Wake the Town..." by Harold W. Kennedy
	Crank, James F.	10	1896	Herman Blatz to James Crank
	El Dorado County Arch	I(A)4	1852-69	Tax Sale Certificates
	El Dorado County Arch	IE114	1852-95	Count Treasurer's Records
	Fernald, Charles	3	1877	Henry M. Newhall to Charles Fernald
	Fernald, Charles	3	1877	H. G. Newhall to Charles Fernald
	Fernald, Charles	3	1878	William Higby (U.S. International Revenue) to Emily Magraw
	Fernald, Charles	4	1880	Henry M. Newhall to Charles Fernald (various)
	Fernald, Charles	4	1880	Henry Newhall to Charles Fernald (various)

Subject Hdgs./ Subdivision	Collection	Box	Date	Finder's Aid
TAXATION (cont.)				
	Fernald, Charles	4	1885	Henry Newhall to Charles Fernald
	Fernald, Charles	4	1886	Henry Newhall to Charles Fernald
	Ford, John Anson	18	1934-58	Los Angeles city assessor papers
	Graves, Jackson A.	11	1918	Jackson A. Graves to I. W. Hellman
	Graves, Jackson A.	11	1921	Jackson A. Graves to E. S. Heller
	Graves, Jackson A.	9	1900	William Denman to H. W. O'Melveny
	Graves, Jackson A.	11	1915	Jackson A. Graves to I. W. Hellman
	Graves, Jackson A.	1	1892	William Staats to H. W. O'Melveny
	Graves, Jackson A.	3	1894	S. D. Rosenbaum to J. A. Graves
	Graves, Jackson A.	2	1894	Clinton Hale to H. W. O'Melveny
	Graves, Jackson A.	2	1894	Carlos Olvera to H. W. O'Melveny
	Graves, Jackson A.	5	1897	Balfour, Guthrie & Co. to Graves
	Graves, Jackson A.	5	1897	O'Melveny and Shankland (various)
	Graves, Jackson A.	7	1898	Carlos Olvera to Henry W. O'Melveny
	Graves, Jackson A.	7	1898	Horace G. Platt to Henry W. O'Melveny
	Graves, Jackson A.	7	1898	Title Insurance & Trust Co. to J. A. Graves, H. W. O'Melveny & J. H. Shankland
	Haight, Henry	6	1870	Samuel S. Marshall to Henry Haight
	Mandeville, James Wylie	2	1853	E. Sawtell to James Mandeville
	Mandeville, James Wylie	7	1856	Eugene Drake to James Mandeville
	Mandeville, James Wylie	8	1857	James McChesney to James Mandeville

Subject Hdgs./ Subdivision	*Collection*	*Box*	*Date*	*Finder's Aid*
TAXATION (cont.)				
	Mandeville, James Wylie	9	1857	Robert McGarvey to James Mandeville
	Mandeville, James Wylie	9	1858	James McChesney to James Mandeville
	Morgan, William Rollin	1	1866	William Thomas to William R. Morgan
	Morgan, William Rollin	2	1882	Daniel Titus to William Morgan
	Morgan, William Rollin	9	1889	Robert Barton to James de Barth Shorb
	Morgan, William Rollin	13	1889	Charles Broaddus to James de Barth Shorb
	Morgan, William Rollin	33	1891	William J. Crossley to James M. Tiernan
	Morgan, William Rollin	41	1885-86	Asa Ellis to James de Barth Shorb
	Morgan, William Rollin	41	1888	Asa Ellis to James de Barth Shorb
	Morgan, William Rollin	41	1889	Asa Ellis to James de Barth Shorb
	Morgan, William Rollin	65	1885	Kohler & Frohling to James de Barth Shorb
	Morgan, William Rollin	68	1897	O. W. Longden to Maria Shorb
	Morgan, William Rollin	73	1888	Robert McPherson to James de Barth Shorb
	Morgan, William Rollin	103	1891	Winfield Scott to James de Barth Shorb
	Morgan, William Rollin	103	1891	Winfield Scott to James de Barth Shorb
	Morgan, William Rollin	122	1889	U. S. Office of Internal Revenue to Asa Ellis
	Morgan, William Rollin	122	1891	U. S. Office of Internal Revenue to James de Barth Shorb

Subject Hdgs./ Subdivision	*Collection*	*Box*	*Date*	*Finder's Aid*
TAXATION (cont.)				
	Morgan, William Rollin	122	1891	U. S. Office of Internal Revenue to Charles A. Wetmore
	Morgan, William Rollin	122	1892	U. S. Office of Internal Revenue, 1st Dist., Cal to James de Barth Shorb
	Morgan, William Rollin	122	1889	William Vandever to James de Barth Shorb
	Morgan, William Rollin	127	1891	George West to James de Barth Shorb
	Morgan, William Rollin	131	1869	Benjamin D. Wilson to James de Barth Shorb
	Morgan, William Rollin	133	1885-86	George W. Wilson to James de Barth Shorb (various)
	Morgan, William Rollin	133	1887	George W. Wilson to Charles Wetmore
	Shorb, James de Barth	9	1889	Robert Barnett to James de Barth Shorb (various)
	Stearns, Abel	1	1859	Frank Ames correspondence
	Stearns, Abel	4	1862	Frank Baker
	Stearns, Abel	18 & 19	1851-70	Cave J. Couts correspondence
	Stearns, Abel	34	1870	John Hill correspondence
	Stearns, Abel	35	1866	Charles Johnson correspondence
	Stearns, Abel	38	1871	James Laidley correspondence
	Stearns, Abel	39	1844	Thomas O. Larkin correspondence
	Stearns, Abel	40	1845-46	Thomas O. Larkin correspondence
	Stearns, Abel	41	1869-71	Timothy Lynch correspondence

Subject Hdgs./ Subdivision	Collection	Box	Date	Finder's Aid
TAXATION (cont.)				
	Stearns, Abel	45	1868	Ephraim W. Morse correspondence
	Stearns, Abel	45	1868-71	Edward Northam correspondence
	Stearns, Abel	48	1857	Eugene Pendleton correspondence
	Stearns, Abel	50	1861	Rufus Porter correspondence
	Stearns, Abel	54-56	1850-73	Alfred Robinson correspondence
	Stearns, Abel	58	1864-71	Horace Rolfe correspondence
	Stearns, Abel	59	1870	John Satterwhite correspondence
	Stearns, Abel	60	1876	William Spurgeon correspondence
	Stimson, Marshall	1	1951	Stimson to Basil Gordon
	Terry, David Smith	3	1882	David Terry to Cornelia Terry
	Watkins, Louise Ward	5	1942	Louise Watkins to Pasy
	Wolfskill, Lewis	5	1875	Board of Ed. of L. A. vs. L. A.
TITLE				
	Jacks, David	BV414	1863	Letter: Jacks & Ashley least to Antonio Mays
	Jacks, David	BV414	1880	Jacks to Rafael Barrales
	Jacks, David	C1	1871	Archie Fraim to Jacks
	Jacks, David	C(3)	1880	John J. Williams to David Jacks
	Jacks, David	C4	1883	S. O. Houghton to Jacks
	Jacks, David	C(5)	1886	David Jacks to S. O. Houghton
	Jacks, David	C(5)	1885	S. O. Houghton to David Jacks
	Jacks, David	C(6)	1888	C. W. Gates to Jacks
	Jacks, David	C(1)	1864	David Jacks to D. R. Ashley
	Jacks, David	C(1)	1866	David Jacks to Hon C. Cole

Subject Hdgs./ Subdivision	Collection	Box	Date	Finder's Aid
TITLE (cont.)				
	Jacks, David	C(1)	1856	Extens. Corres. on Ranch Chualar; Letter of Britton & Fray to W. H. Patterson (Attys.)
	Jacks, David	C(1)	1872	Extens. Corres. on Ranch Chualar; Letter of Britton & Fray to W. H. Patterson (Attys.)
	Jacks, David	C(1)	1872	Houghton & Reynolds to David Jacks
	Jacks, David	C(2)	1878	David Jacks to Hon. Thomas Flint
	Jacks, David	C(1)	1869	James F. Stuart to David Jacks, 11/29/69
	Jacks, David	C(1)	1869	William Irvine to David Jacks
	Jacks, David	BV211		Litigation of Title
	Jones, Elbert P.	1	1868	Micheal Bulke to Joseph J. & Sarah Jones
	Keller, Matthew	1	1877	George Hansen to Matthew Keller
	Markham, H. H.	7	1890	L. T. Garnsey to H. H. Markham
	Markham, H. H.	4	1886	F. H. Colton to H. H. Markham
	New Almaden Mine	1	1858-62	Law Firm note book includes cases newspaper clippings, notes
	O'Farrell, Jasper	1		Survey of ranchoes & SF streets
	Potter, Charles & Isaac	4	1919-20	Mono Power Co. (various)
	Potter, Charles & Isaac	6	1905-30	Southern Sierra Power Co (various)
	Price, Rodman M.	1	1850	E. O. Carter (S.F.) to Samuel Ward
	Price, Rodman M.		1850	Augustus J. Bowie to Edward Curtis

Subject Hdgs./ Subdivision	*Collection*	*Box*	*Date*	*Finder's Aid*
TITLE (cont.)				
	Wolter, Charles		1851	Chas. H. St. John (S.F.) to Chas. Wolter
Agriculture	Jacks, David	BV414	1860	Jacks to Manuel Apezarena
Agriculture	Jacks, David	BV414	1909	Jacks & Ashley to Rutherford
Agriculture	Jacks, David	BIII8	1872	266 acres (Jacks) to D. Hargins
Agriculture	Jacks, David	BV414	1880	Jacks to Antonil & Manual Rodgers
Agriculture	Jacks, David	BV414	1862	D. R. Ashley & Jacks to Jose Botellen
Agriculture	Jacks, David	C6	1887	C. S. Gates to Jacks
Agriculture	Jacks, David	BV414		Jacks to Pedro Gonzales
TORTS				
	Bowron, Fletcher	42	1961	Law of Governmental Tort Immunity by Harold W. Kennedy
	Bowron, Fletcher	42	1962	Unlimited Tort Liability by Harold W. Kennedy
	Bowron, Fletcher	42	1962	Accident and Liability Avoidance in Public Agencies by H. W. Kennedy
	Bowron, Fletcher	42	1963	Recent Developments by Harold W. Kennedy and Robert Lynch
	Graves, Jackson A.	3	1895	Chino Valley Beet Sugar Co to H. W. O'Melveny (various)
	Graves, Jackson A.	3	1894	W. H. Shinn to N. H. Cottman
Defamation	Shorb, James de Barth	49	1892	Graves, O'Melveny & Shankland to James de Barth Shorb

Subject Hdgs./ Subdivision	*Collection*	*Box*	*Date*	*Finder's Aid*
TORTS (cont.)				
Insurance	Graves, Jackson A.	3	1895	A. F. Morrison to Henry O'Melveny
Libel	Graves, Jackson A.	7	1898	Stephen White to Henry O'Melveny on *Patton v. Herald Publishing Co.*
Railroad	Fernald, Charles	3	1875	John P. Green to Charles Fernald
Railroad	Fernald, Charles	3	1876	D. N. Welch to Charles Fernald
Sovereign Immnty	Bowron, Fletcher	42	1962	Harold W. Kennedy to Edwin Regan
Wrongful Death	Graves, Jackson A.	5	1896	Southern Pacific RR to J. A. Graves, H. W. O'Melveny & J. H. Shankland
Wrongful Death	Graves, Jackson A.	7	1898	Miller & Brown to J. A. Graves, H. W. O'Melveny & J. H. Shankland
WATER				
	Azusa-Foothill Cit.	1	1902	Covina Irrigating Co. documents
	Barclay, Henry	4	1872	Rancho Muscu-piabe (various)
	Barclay, Henry	5	1885	Wilson, Robert N. C. Claim in San Bernardino County
	Barclay, Henry	5	1885	Hancock, John, Water Notice on East Twin Creek, San Bernardino Co., 2/15/1885
	Barclay, Henry	5	1885	Barclay, H. A. to John H. Caruth-ers, Opinion of Water Rights
	Barclay, Henry	5	1893	Barclay, H. A. Water Claim to Big Tujunga Canon (various)
	Barclay, Henry	5	1897	Young, Frank C. Water Claim to Big Tujunga Canon

Subject Hdgs./ Subdivision	*Collection*	*Box*	*Date*	*Finder's Aid*
WATER (cont.)				
	Barclay, Henry	5	1895	John S. Chapman to Lytle Creek Water and Improvement Co., Opinion Letter
	Bard, Thomas R.	7C-D	1900s	Irrigation & arid lands
	Bard, Thomas R.	9B	1900s	Misc. irrigation papers
	Bowron, Fletcher	42	1960	"Federal Claims Against California's Unappropriated Water" by Harold W. Kennedy, County Counsel
	Bowron, Fletcher	42	1960	"Legal Background of Water Supply in Southern Cal." by Harold W. Kennedy
	Bowron, Fletcher	42	1961	"Future Availability of Water for Southern California" by Harold W. Kennedy
	Bowron, Fletcher	42	1962	Accident and Liability Avoidance by Harold W. Kennedy & Lloyd Davis
	Bowron, Fletcher	42	1962	Quieting Title to Western Waters by Harold W. Kennedy
	Bowron, Fletcher	42	1963	Special Report by Harold W. Kennedy
	Bowron, Fletcher	42	1963	Federal Claims v. State Water Rights by Harold Kennedy
	Catlin, Amos P.	4		Reg. of Am. River Water & Mining Co., re: Mining Claims

Subject Hdgs./ Subdivision	Collection	Box	Date	Finder's Aid
WATER (cont.)				
	Catlin, Amos P.	2	1854-55	Acknowledgement of Deed; Am. River Wtr & Mining Co., releases & assignments of water rights
	Center, John	4	1863	Centerville Mining & Water Co. Claim to Owens River
	Center, John	4	1863	George Phillips to John Center
	Center, John	4	1863	J. W. Phillips to George Phillips
	Center, John	4	1863	Centerville Mining & Water Co.
	Center, John	4	1863	J. W. Phillips to John Center
	Crank, James F.	7	1898	S. P. Jewett to Albert F. Crank
	Dalton, Henry	14	1866-83	Rancho Azusa water rights papers
	Fernald, Charles	3	1876	N. W. Blanchard to Charles Fernald (various)
	Fernald, Charles	3	1876	Alex F. Maclure to Charles Fernald
	Fernald, Charles	3	1877	N. W. Blanchard to Charles Fernald (various)
	Fernald, Charles	4	1885	Nathan Blanchard to Charles Fernald
	Fernald, Charles	4	1887	Timothy Hopkins to Charles Fernald (various)
	Fernald, Charles	4	1888	Timothy Hopkins to Charles Fernald
	Fernald, Charles	4	1889	Blackstock & Shepard to T. R. Bard
	Fernald, Charles	5	1891	Robert Y. Hayne to Charles Fernald
	Fernald, Charles	5	1890	Charles Fernald to Thomas Bard
	Ford, John Anson	9	1936-57	Los Angeles water papers

Subject Hdgs./ Subdivision	Collection	Box	Date	Finder's Aid
WATER (cont.)				
	Graves, Jackson A.	11	1920	Jackson A. Graves to H. W. Keller
	Graves, Jackson A.	11	1924	Jackson A. Graves to various
	Graves, Jackson A.	11	1924	Jackson A. Graves to various regarding Ownes Valley litigation
	Graves, Jackson A.	11	1918	Jackson A. Graves to W. W. Watterson regarding Ownes Valley litigation
	Graves, Jackson A.	11	1918	W. W. Watterson to J. A. Graves regarding Ownes Valley litigation
	Graves, Jackson A.	9	1900	Charles Silent to H. W. O'Melveny
	Graves, Jackson A.	11	1919	Jackson A. Graves to I. W. Hellman
	Graves, Jackson A.	10	1901	Goodrich & McCutchen to H. W. O'Melveny
	Graves, Jackson A.	1	1892	J. M. Jones to Graves, O'Melveny & Shankland
	Graves, Jackson A.	1	1893	Curtis, Oster, & Curtis to Graves, O'Melveny & Shankland
	Graves, Jackson A.	2	1894	Isaias Hellman to J. A. Graves
	Graves, Jackson A.	5	1897	Freemen & Bates to J. A. Graves, H. W. O'Melveny & J. H. Shankland
	Graves, Jackson A.	88-90	1888-90	Graves, O'Melveny & Shankland to James O'Reilly
	Graves, Jackson A.	88-90	1890	Wright Irrigation Act; Bonds
	Graves, Jackson A.	7	1898	M. H. Sherman to J. A. Graves on Owens Valley Water Project
	Heslop Family	1	1893	Jose Heslop to L. J. Rose contract

Subject Hdgs./ Subdivision	Collection	Box	Date	Finder's Aid
WATER (cont.)				
	Hoadley, Milo	1	1860	Hoadley to Islais & Salinas Water Works
	Hoadley, Milo	1	1870	Hoadley to Editors of Alta
	Hoadley, Milo	1	1870	Hoadley to various
	Hoadley, Milo	2	1850-56	Hoadley's field notes incl. memo on S. F. water needs
	Keller, Matthew	3	1871	Keller, Matthew to editors, Alta
	Kincade, John T.	1	1850	John Kincade to James Kincade
	Kincade, John T.	1	1850	G. A. Cassil to James & Hannah Kincade
	Kincade, John T.	1	1852	John Kincade to James Kincade
	Mandeville, James Wylie	5	1855	Edgar Mills to James Mandeville
	Mandeville, James Wylie	6	1856	Leander Quint to James Mandeville
	Markham, H. H.	9	1890	J. M. Hurley to H. H. Markham (various)
	Markham, H. H.	10	1897	Edwin Lamme to H. H. Markham
	Markham, H. H.	13	1896	Maurice H. Newmark to H. H. Markham
	Morgan, William Rollin	2	1886	James Jones to J. H. Thomas
	Potter, Charles & Isaac	1	1916-26	Cain Irrigation Co. & Pacific Power Corp. (various)
	Potter, Charles & Isaac	1	1916-33	Cain Irrigation Co., v. Cain, Amiot, et al. water rights litigation papers
	Potter, Charles & Isaac	2	1919-22	Cal-Nevada Canal, Water & Power Co. (various)

Subject Hdgs./ Subdivision	*Collection*	*Box*	*Date*	*Finder's Aid*
WATER (cont.)				
	Potter, Charles & Isaac	2	1918-20	Rush Creek Mutual Ditch Co., et al. v. Cal-Nevada Canal, Water & Power Co. (administrative proceedings — various)
	Potter, Charles & Isaac	3	1909-24	Hillside Water Co. (various)
	Potter, Charles & Isaac	4	1919-37	Mono Power Company (various)
	Potter, Charles & Isaac	5	1905-08	Nevada-Calif. Electric Co. (various) [includes suit against Theo. Roosevelt]
	Potter, Charles & Isaac	5	1919-21	Cain Irrigation Co. [Grant Lake Reservoir] (various)
	Potter, Charles & Isaac	6	1924	A. B. West To L. C. Phipps (various)
	Potter, Charles & Isaac	6	1905-30	Southern Sierra Power Co (various)
	Potter, Charles & Isaac	7	1905-21	Southern Sierra Power Co. [Fish Slough Project in Mono & Inyo Counties] (various)
	Potter, Charles & Isaac	7	1913	Chas. F. Potter to Delos A. Chappell (various)
	Potter, Charles & Isaac	7	1905	Notices of Appropriation
	Potter, Charles & Isaac	7	1914-18	Southern Sierra Power Co. (various) [Cottonwood Creek Water and Power Development]
	Potter, Charles & Isaac	7	1918	Southern Sierra v. Schoba, et al. and Tulare v. Dinuba cases

Subject Hdgs./ Subdivision	*Collection*	*Box*	*Date*	*Finder's Aid*
WATER (cont.)				
	Potter, Charles & Isaac	7	1921-22	Water Power Act correspondence
	Potter, Charles & Isaac	7	1913	Chas. F. Potter to Consaul & Heltman (various)
	Shorb, James de Barth	1	1891-93	Alhambra Addition Water Co. to James de Barth Shorb
	Shorb, James de Barth	2	1883	H. M. Ames to James de Barth Shorb
	Shorb, James de Barth	6	1890	Mother Superior Augustin to James de Barth Shorb
	Shorb, James de Barth	7	1888	Baker Iron Works to James de Barth Shorb
	Shorb, James de Barth	7	1892	Thomas Banbury to James de Barth Shorb
	Shorb, James de Barth	8	1886	Thomas Bard to James de Barth Shorb
	Shorb, James de Barth	10	1888	John D. Bicknell to James de Barth Shorb
	Shorb, James de Barth	11	1892	Rufus F. Bishop to James de Barth Shorb (various)
	Shorb, James de Barth	11	1885	Thomas Benton Bishop to James de Barth Shorb
	Shorb, James de Barth	19	1884-89	William B. Carr to James de Barth Shorb (various)
	Shorb, James de Barth	22	1886-88	Clark Churchill to James de Barth Shorb (various)
	Shorb, James de Barth	23	1888-93	Clark Churchill to James de Barth Shorb (various)
	Shorb, James de Barth	24	1890	Coit, Barton, & Cowles to James de Barth Shorb (various)
	Shorb, James de Barth	28	1884	William T. Coleman to James de Barth Shorb

Subject Hdgs./ Subdivision	Collection	Box	Date	Finder's Aid
WATER (cont.)				
	Shorb, James de Barth	31	1885	William T. Coleman to James de Barth Shorb
	Shorb, James de Barth	40	1889	Benjamin S. Eaton to James de Barth Shorb
	Shorb, James de Barth	40	1886	Eugene E. Edwards to James de Barth Shorb
	Shorb, James de Barth	41	1886	Asa Ellis to James de Barth Shorb
	Shorb, James de Barth	41	1886	Morris M. Estee to James de Barth Shorb
	Shorb, James de Barth	47	1891	Richard Garvey to M. Shorb
	Shorb, James de Barth	49	1892	Jackson A. Graves to James de Barth Shorb
	Shorb, James de Barth	49	1892	Graves, O'Melveny & Shankland to James de Barth Shorb
	Shorb, James de Barth	50	1884	Will S. Green to James de Barth Shorb
	Shorb, James de Barth	51	1886	Brice Grimes to James de Barth Shorb
	Shorb, James de Barth	51	1886	T. G. Haines to James de Barth Shorb
	Shorb, James de Barth	52	1891	William H. Hall to Francis G. Newlands
	Shorb, James de Barth	52	1886	William H. Hall to James de Barth Shorb
	Shorb, James de Barth	54	1897	Charles T. Healey to Maria Shorb
	Shorb, James de Barth	57	1886	Tobias Hock to James de Barth Shorb
	Shorb, James de Barth	58	1886	A. K. Holt to James de Barth Shorb

Subject Hdgs./ Subdivision	Collection	Box	Date	Finder's Aid
WATER (cont.)				
	Shorb, James de Barth	58	1884-92	Luther M. Holt to James de Barth Shorb (various)
	Shorb, James de Barth	58	1885	Casper T. Hopkins to James de Barth Shorb
	Shorb, James de Barth	58	1890-91	Casper T. Hopkins to James de Barth Shorb
	Shorb, James de Barth	59	1890	Charles Webb Howard to James de Barth Shorb
	Shorb, James de Barth	60	1885-86	R. Hudnut to James de Barth Shorb (various)
	Shorb, James de Barth	61	1886	John P. Irish to James de Barth Shorb
	Shorb, James de Barth	63	1892	Keese & Lawrence to James de Barth Shorb
	Shorb, James de Barth	64	1885	Abbot Kinney to James de Barth Shorb
	Shorb, James de Barth	65	1886	Henry L. Knight to James de Barth Shorb
	Shorb, James de Barth	73	1884	William H. McKee to James de Barth Shorb
	Shorb, James de Barth	73	1886	William H. McKee to Maria Shorb
	Shorb, James de Barth	73	1886	Elisha W. McKinstry to James de Barth Shorb
	Shorb, James de Barth	74	1886	Henry Harrison Markhanm to James de Barth Shorb
	Shorb, James de Barth	74	1886	Bernard Marks to James de Barth Shorb
	Shorb, James de Barth	98	1884	L. H. Rodgers to James de Barth Shorb

Subject Hdgs./ Subdivision	*Collection*	*Box*	*Date*	*Finder's Aid*
WATER (cont.)				
	Shorb, James de Barth	100	1891	H. J. Rudisill to James de Barth Shorb
	Shorb, James de Barth	105	1888	James de Barth Shorb to William, Christy
	Shorb, James de Barth	105	1886	James de Barth Shorb to Creed Haymond
	Shorb, James de Barth	106	1892-93	James de Barth Shorb to Los Angeles City Water Co. (various)
	Shorb, James de Barth	81	1886	Francis Newlands to James de Barth Shorb (8/5/86)
	Shorb, James de Barth	82	1889	Francis Newlands to James de Barth Shorb
	Shorb, James de Barth	83	1884	John Wesley North to James de Barth Shorb (various)
	Shorb, James de Barth	91	1886	Henry W. Patton to James de Barth Shorb (various)
	Shorb, James de Barth	115	1886	Phillip Stein to James de Barth Shorb
	Shorb, James de Barth	116	1890	Emanuel Stern to James de Barth Shorb
	Shorb, James de Barth	78	1889	William R. Morrow to James de Barth Shorb
	Shorb, James de Barth	79	1891-92	Leroy E. Mosher to James de Barth Shorb (various)
	Shorb, James de Barth	79	1889	Frank M. Mott to James de Barth Shorb
	Shorb, James de Barth	93	1892	Edward F. Phlean to James de Barth Shorb
	Shorb, James de Barth	95	1890-92	Gervaise Purcell to James de Barth Shorb (various)

Subject Hdgs./ Subdivision	Collection	Box	Date	Finder's Aid
WATER (cont.)				
	Shorb, James de Barth	102	1890-93	James D. Schuyler to James de Barth Shorb (various)
	Shorb, James de Barth	110	1894	Herman Silver to James de Barth Shorb
	Shorb, James de Barth	117	1892-93	Harriet Strong to James de Barth Shorb (various)
	Shorb, James de Barth	118	1891	Charles Sumner to James M. Tiernan
	Shorb, James de Barth	118	1892-93	James T. Taylor to James de Barth Shorb (various)
	Shorb, James de Barth	110	1894	Herman Silver to James de Barth Shorb
	Shorb, James de Barth	117	1892-93	Harriet Strong to James de Barth Shorb (various)
	Shorb, James de Barth	118	1891	Charles Sumner to James M. Tiernan
	Shorb, James de Barth	118	1892-93	James T. Taylor to James de Barth Shorb (various)
	Shorb, James de Barth	121	1886	E. H. Tucker to James de Barth Shorb
	Shorb, James de Barth	123	1884	F. H. Wales to James de Barth Shorb
	Shorb, James de Barth	124	1886	Byron Waters to James de Barth Shorb
	Shorb, James de Barth	126	1886	J. H. G. Weaver to James de Barth Shorb
	Shorb, James de Barth	127	1884	George West to James de Barth Shorb
	Shorb, James de Barth	128	1884-86	J. F. Wharton to James de Barth Shorb (various)
	Shorb, James de Barth	128	1886	Stephen M. White to James de Barth Shorb (various)

Subject Hdgs./ Subdivision	Collection	Box	Date	Finder's Aid
WATER (cont.)				
	Shorb, James de Barth	130	1885	P. D. Wiggington to James de Barth Shorb
	Shorb, James de Barth	131	1869-75	Benjamin D. Wilson to James de Barth Shorb (various)
	Shorb, James de Barth	132	1869	Benjamin D. Wilson to Maria Shorb (various)
	Shorb, James de Barth	133	1891	John W. Wilson to James de Barth Shorb (various)
	Shorb, James de Barth	134	1892	Robert N. C. Wilson to Erskine M. Ross
	Shorb, James de Barth	134	1878	Frederick W. Wood to James de Barth Shorb (various)
	Shorb, James de Barth	135	1885-86	Frederick W. Wood to James de Barth Shorb (various)
	Shorb, James de Barth	136	1886	Frederick W. Wood to James de Barth Shorb (various)
	Shorb, James de Barth	136	1878	Frederick W. Wood to Benjamin D. Wilson
	Wolfskill, Lewis	5	1875	Beaudry & Desnoyers to L. A. Common Council
	Wolfskill, Lewis	5	1875	Wilfskill judgment in L. A. Co.
	Wolfskill, Lewis	6	1877	Cajon Irrigation Co. to Wolfskill
	Wolfskill, Lewis	6	1877	Henry Dalton to Lewis Wolfskill
	Shorb, James de Barth	1	1888	J. C. Abbot to James de Barth Shorb
	Graves, Jackson A.	10	1901	George Fuller to John E. Boal

Subject Hdgs./ Subdivision	*Collection*	*Box*	*Date*	*Finder's Aid*
WATER (cont.)				
Contract	Graves, Jackson A.	10	1901	Edward R. Annable to Graves, O'Melveny and Shankland
Contract	Shorb, James de Barth	1	1889	James M. Allen to James de Barth Shorb
Deed	Barclay, Henry	5	1895	Blackington, S. C. to Barclay, H. A., Los Angeles County
Deed	Barclay, Henry	5	1892	Hotchkiss & Daniel to Grapeland Irrigation District, San Bernardino
Deed	Graves, Jackson A.	9	1900	J. B. Reinstein to Graves, O'Melveny and Shankland
Deed	Markham, H. H.	4	1895	John S. Chapman to H. H. Markham
Deed	Shorb, James de Barth	106	1883	James de Barth Shorb to Bishop Francis Mora
Deed	Graves, Jackson A.	88-90 LB	1888	J. A. Graves to Mrs. Mary O. H. Stoneman. Inspection of deeds in response to complaint about employee
Easement	Markham, H. H.	2	1896	Charles E. Brooks to H. H. Markham
Eminent Domain	Shorb, James de Barth	47	1886	J. B. Furney to James de Barth Shorb
Estate	Graves, Jackson A.	11	1918	Jackson A. Graves to I. W. Hellman
Mortgage	Shorb, James de Barth	103	1891	Security Loan & Trust Co. to S. V. Landt
Mortgage	Shorb, James de Barth	103	1891	Security Loan & Trust Co. to S. V. Landt

Subject Hdgs./ Subdivision	*Collection*	*Box*	*Date*	*Finder's Aid*
WATER (cont.)				
	Barclay, Henry	5	1886	East Side Water Co. of L. A.
Pollution	Morgan, William Rollin	2	1885	George W. Cox to William Morgan
Pollution	Morgan, William Rollin	2	1886	George W. Cox to William Morgan
Rates	Shorb, James de Barth	55	1889	William F. Herrin to James de Barth Shorb

COLLECTION DESCRIPTIONS

ADAMS & COMPANY
750 pieces, 1851-ca.1885

Adams & Company was a California branch of the eastern express firm of Adams & Company, founded in Boston in 1840. Successful throughout the state in the express and banking business, it was run by Daniel Hale Haskell and Isaiah Churchill Woods, with Adams as a special partner. The company closed down when the financial crisis of February, 1855 forced it into receivership and numerous legal problems followed.

This is a significant collection. The scrapbooks are excellent resources. Debtor/creditor documents abound in the collection. The letterbook of Adams and Company in box 1 is useful for business history as well as legal history. Other documents concern chiefly the years following the failures of Adams & Co. (1855-1863), especially as they affected Alfred A. Cohen, appointed first receiver of the company; Cohen's business and legal associations (1864-1884) with the Central Pacific Railroad Co.; 1876 trial, Central Pacific Railroad Co. vs. Alfred A. Cohen.

Subject Headings:
Banking
Commercial Law
Contracts
Crimes
Debtor & Creditor
Landlord & Tenant

Law & Practice
Real Property
Taxation

ARAM, JOSEPH (ca.1810-ca.1898)
90 pieces, 1835-1912

Joseph Aram, pioneer resident of Santa Clara County, came to California with his family from Illinois in 1846. He served as a captain in the Mexican War, as a delegate to the first California Constitutional Convention, and as a member of the first state legislature. He established the first tree nursery in San Jose, where he lived from 1849-1898.

This collection is of marginal significance. Some letters touch on mortgages and crime.

Subject Headings:
Crimes
Labor
Land Practice
Natural Resources
Real Property

AZUSA-FOOTHILL CITRUS COMPANY
59 pieces, 1844-1956

The Azusa-Foothill Citrus Company was established in 1902 by James Slauson and his two sisters on property inherited from their father, Jonathan Sayre Slauson, New York banker and founder and manager of the Los Angeles Savings Bank. The land, originally part of the great Azusa Ranch owned by Henry Dalton, was purchased in 1880 and 1884 by Jonathan Sayre Slauson, who founded the town of Azusa, California and the Azusa Land and Water Co.

This collection is of marginal significance. The land papers are of interest and the company papers of 1902-1908 could be of interest for business history. The documents generally concern business and legal afairs of the Azusa Foothill Citrus Co., including copies of title abstracts for Ranchos Azusa, San Jose, and Addition; minute books for the Azusa Land and Water Co., Azusa Citrus Association, and the Azusa Foothill Citrus Co.; and maps showing land and water distribution, irrigation systems, and roads for the period 1878-1937.

Subject Headings:
Agriculture
Corporations
Real Property
Water

BACON, HENRY DOUGLAS (1817-1893)
approximately 4,000 pieces, ca.1766-1906

Henry Douglas Bacon was a California financier who entered the retail business in St. Louis in 1835 and later joined his wealthy father-in-law in the banking firm of Page & Bacon. In 1849 he and his partners formed Page, Bacon & Co., an express firm in San Francisco, which became primarily a banking concern. The company's failure in 1855 served as a prelude to the San Francisco crash of 1855. Bacon invested in the Ohio & Mississippi Railroad, numerous mining ventures, and the Marengo Ranch in Southern California (1871-1873). He donated generously to the University of California at Berkeley.

This is a significant collection. The banking correspondence in boxes 2-7 span the period 1852-1863 and contain useful information and insights. Other documents concern banking methods in the 1850s, the failure of Page & Bacon and Page & Co.; the financing of the Ohio & Mississippi Railroad; land transactions in Missouri and Illinois; mines and mining properties in the western states; the wine and citrus industries in Southern California; the Los Angeles and San

Gabriel Valley Railroad; the purchase, boundaries, and subdivision of the Marengo Ranch (now South Pasadena, California); the construction of the Raymond Hotel in Pasadena.

Subject Headings:
Agriculture
Banking
Debtor & Creditor
Real Property

BAKER, ROBERT SYMINGTON (1825-1894)
320 pieces, 1866-1890

Robert S. Baker, California businessman, came to California in 1849 from his birthplace in Rhode Island. Arriving in San Diego, he went next to San Francisco, then settled in Los Angeles. He was prominently associated with Edward P. Beale in the local petroleum and wool industries and also engaged in mining, banking, and real estate. Baker married Arcadia Bandini de Stearns (widow of Abel Stearns) in 1874 and later built the Baker Block in downtown Los Angeles. He owned Ranchos San Vicente and Santa Monica and, with John Percival Jones, founded the city of Santa Monica.

This is a moderately significant collection. The land papers and correspondence concerning oil are of particular interest. Several letters of Charles Forbes raise issues of constitutional law. Other documents concern petroleum and sheep and wool industries in California, 1866-1888; mining interests in California and Utah, 1877-1879; the city of Santa Monica, 1877-1879; the ranchos Jurupa, Santa Monica, San Vicente, and Temescal. Other legal topics include commercial law, debtor and creditor, taxation, family law, and law practice.

Subject Headings:
Commercial Law
Constitutional Law
Contracts

Debtor & Creditor
Law & Practice
Natural Resources
Real Property
Taxation

BALDWIN, ANITA MAY (1876-1939)
approximately 600 pieces, 1876-1936

Anita M. Baldwin was the daughter of Elias Jackson ("Lucky") Baldwin (1828-1909), millionaire investor in Comstock mining stocks and later developer of the Santa Anita Rancho, which he bought from Harris Newmark in 1875. After Baldwin's death, Anita Baldwin inherited the ranch (including vineyards, orchards, livestock, and race horses), which she continued to run until selling several acres to the Los Angeles Turf Club in 1933 and most of the remaining acreage for subdivision in 1936.

This collection is marginally significant. The real property and estate papers are of some interest. Other documents concern business affairs of the Santa Anita Ranch (1901-1904), and the Los Angeles Racing Association (1907-1922); business affairs of Anita M. Baldwin and estate settlements of Elias Jackson Baldwin and his elder daughter Clara (Baldwin) Stocker, covering the period 1876-1936, including two volumes of Arcadia (California) city dockets on Criminal and Civil justice.

Subject Headings:
Corporations
Crimes
Debtor & Creditor
Estates
Family Law
Natural Resources
Real Property

BARCLAY, HENRY AUGUSTUS (1849-1920)
approximately 150 pieces, 1867-1908

Henry A. Barclay, Los Angeles lawyer, was born in Pennsylvania, engaged in surveying work as a young man, and came to California in 1874. He began his practice of law in Los Angeles in 1875 and dealt mainly in land law, including Spanish and Mexican land grants.

This is a moderately significant collection containing land papers. The collection also contains some documents of interest in water law research. Other documents involve coal, gold, and silver mining in California and Mexico; the Irvington Land and Water Co.; San Bernardino; the Los Angeles Light and Water Co.; and several Southern California Ranchos (including Muscupiabe, San Bernardino, Sespe, and Tujunga). Other topics include real property (mortgage) and corporations.

Subject Headings:
Contracts
Corporations
Landlord & Tenant
Real property
Water

BARD, THOMAS ROBERT (1841-1915)
approximately 50,000 pieces, 1866-1958

Thomas Robert Bard, U.S. senator from California from 1900-1905 and president of the Union Oil Company, was born in Pennsylvania where he studied law. He came to California in 1865 to take charge of the large land holdings of eastern owners in Ventura County and was instrumental in the subsequent development of land and petroleum. Bard laid out the town of Hueneme, California, and was involved in many Ventura County business ventures.

This is a significant collection. There is a massive amount of material about the oil industry that no student of that industry or business history can avoid. The collection also contains useful materials on irrigation in boxes 7 C-D and 9 B. Documents generally concern the Union Oil Company, its subsidiaries, and other enterprises with which Bard was concerned; local and national politics from 1870 to 1915; the development of Ventura County; business papers (1909-1958) of the Quimichis Colony, an American-financed agricultural company in Nayarit, Mexico, of which Richard Bard (son of Thomas R. Bard) was president.

Subject Headings:
Contracts
Natural Resources
Real Property
Water

BELL, HORACE (1830-1918)
71 pieces, 1829-1890

Horace Bell, pioneer Los Angeles resident, came to California in 1850 to engage in mining and settled in Los Angeles in 1852. Bell joined the Rangers, a local group formed to provide law and order, and later wrote *Reminiscences of a Ranger*, describing his experiences in early Los Angeles. He saw military service in 1856 with General William Walker in Nicaragua, in 1859 with Benito Juarez in Mexico, and in the Civil War. Bell returned to Los Angeles, where he practiced law and published a weekly newspaper, *The Porcupine*.

This collection is of marginal significance containing some correspondence regarding real estate. Other topics of interest concern lawyers and law practice.

Subject Headings:
Law & Practice
Real Property

BOWRON, FLETCHER (1887-1968)
approximately 20,000 pieces, 1934-1970

Fletcher Bowron, mayor of Los Angeles from 1938 to 1953, came into office as a reform candidate in a recall election and served during a period of unusual growth and problems. Bowron had been a newspaper reporter, practiced law, and spent six years as a judge of the Superior Court of Los Angeles County. Following his term as mayor, Bowron was reelected judge of the Superior Court. After retirement he became interested in the study of Los Angeles history and initiated the Metropolitan Los Angeles History Project, which produced the bibliographical work, *Los Angeles and Its Environs in the Twentieth Century*.

This is a significant collection particularly for an understanding of Los Angeles municipal government. Of specific interest is the developing law of tort. Several legal opinions by Harold W. Kennedy provide substantial insight into the growing liability exposure of cities as governmental immunities crumble. Other topics in the collection include environment, crime, contract, labor, and taxation.

Subject Headings:
Constitutional Law
Contracts
Crimes
Environmental Law
Labor
Law & Practice
Municipalities
Real Property
Taxation
Torts
Water

BRENT, JOSEPH LANCASTER (1826-1905)
460 pieces, 1850-1939

Joseph L. Brent, lawyer and Confederate officer, was born in

Maryland. In 1850 he settled in Los Angeles, where he held various public offices between 1851 and 1854. He also served as a lawyer before the Land Commission for the Verdugo Rancho and for the City of Los Angeles and was prominent in the Lugo trial (1851). From 1856 to 1860 he was a state legislator. At the outbreak of the Civil War he joined the Confederacy, serving first under John B. Magruder and then under Richard Taylor as chief of ordinance and artillery. His notable military feat was leading the expedition that captured the Union ironclad "Indianola" in 1863. Following the war Brent traveled in Europe, managed a sugar plantation in Louisiana, practiced law in Baltimore, and wrote on national issues.

This is a moderately significant collection with numerous documents dealing with criminal matters including correspondence, Brent's "Life in California," and the Lugo trial. Other topics include real property and estate.

Subject Headings:
Crimes
Real Property

BROPHY-BEESON COLLECTION
240 pieces, 1827-1900

John Brophy (? - 1866) came to California in 1849, engaged in mining, and purchased land in Yuba County from early pioneer John Rose before bringing his family to settle in the west. He participated in Democratic politics and prospered in ranching until about 1857, when he suffered reverses, and subsequently moved to a farm in Oregon in 1865. John Beeson (1803-1889) brought his family from Illinois to Oregon in 1853 and took up farming. Beeson's distress at the cruel treatment of the Indians caused him to go east to write and lecture on their behalf in 1856. John Beeson's son, Welborn Beeson, married John Brophy's daughter and continued the management of the family farm and served in the Oregon Militia.

This is a moderately significant collection. Documents concern gold mining and ranching in Yuba County in the 1850s and disputed California land titles.

Subject Headings
Natural Resources
Real Property

BURNETT, WELLINGTON CLEVELAND (1828-1907)
869 pieces, 1830-1935

Wellington C. Burnett was born in Connecticut of colonial ancestry. He left home at the age of seventeen, joined the U.S. Army, and received a commission after service in the Mexican War (1846-1848). Burnett then attended Harvard Law School, practiced in Chicago, and in 1852 came to California, where he served as state senator for Yuba and Yolo Counties from 1855 to 1857. In 1859 he began the practice of law in San Francisco and was elected city and county attorney of San Francisco in 1869.

This is a marginally significant collection. Documents concern Burnett and his family (1843-1917), articles about early California, and a journal containing an account of Burnett's experiences as a soldier during the Mexican War.

Subject Headings
Law & Practice

BUSINESS WOMEN'S LEGISLATIVE COUNCIL OF CALIFORNIA
approximately 150 pieces, 1927-1943

The Business Women's Legislative Council of California was organized to bring about and maintain, under the law, equal business opportunities for men and women. This marginally significant collection contains documents on women.

CATLIN, AMOS PARMALEE (1823-1900)
approximately 2,760 pieces, 1849-1871

Amos P. Catlin was a lawyer from New York State who came to California in 1849, engaged in mining operations in the Mormon Island area, and later formed the American River Water and Mining Co,. and the Natoma Water and Mining Co. During the 1860s he was associated with the assay and banking firm of Charles T. H. Palmer and Roger S. Day. Catlin, a member of the California bar for many years, was influential in establishing the state capital at Sacramento. He was elected to the state senate in 1852 and judge of the Superior Court at Sacramento in 1890.

This collection is of marginal significance except for American River Water and Mining Co. documents in boxes 2 and 4. Documents concern mining in the Mormon Island area, activities of the American River Water and Mining Co. and the Natoma Water and Mining Co., and operations of the assay and banking firm of Palmer and Day.

Subject Headings:
Admiralty
Real Property
Water

CENTER, JOHN (1817-1908)
362 pieces, 1849-1884

John Center came from Wisconsin to California in 1849 to seek his fortune in gold, but instead settled in San Francisco, becoming involved in many enterprises, including the nursery business, real estate, and mining speculation. Center promoted the expansion and civic improvement of San Francisco, especially in the Mission District. In 1863 he established a mining company in the Owens Valley.

This is a moderately significant collection. The documents making up this collection primarily deal with litigation over land and real estate transactions, debtor/creditor relations, and contract matters. In particular, the land papers contain substantial material dealing with litigation over private land grants, the fee arrangements of lawyers representing land claimants, and the legal strategies used by lawyers to press the claims of their clients (including the lobbying of members of Congress).

Other papers concern the gardening business, real estate and mining transactions, and civil enterprises in San Francisco from 1849 to 1884; papers regarding The Center Company deal with mining and water in the Owens Valley in 1863. Other legal topics include negotiable instruments and landlord and tenant.

Subject Headings:
Agriculture
Commercial Law
Contracts
Debtor & Creditor
Estates
Landlord & Tenant
Law & Practice
Municipalities
Natural Resources
Real Property

CHIPMAN-DWINELLE COLLECTION
approximately 435 pieces, 1845-1943

William Worthington Chipman (1820?-1866), an attorney, with Gideon Aughinbaugh as partner, laid out the city of Alameda, California. The partners had first subleased the land from two Frenchmen in 1850, then purchased the entire Rancho Encinal San Antonio from its original owner, Luis Maria Peralta, in 1851. Following the death of William W. Chipman, his widow, Caroline E. Chipman, married John Whipple Dwinelle (1816-1861), San Francisco lawyer and historian, who practiced law in San Francisco for thirty years and was one of the organizers of the San Francisco Bar Association. Dwinelle lived in Oakland and represented Alameda County in the state assembly.

This is a significant collection. The land papers for Rancho Encinal San Antonio are extensive and the collection also contains significant documents dealing with the prolonged litigation over San Francisco's pueblo title. Other documents concern the defense of titles in the Encinal San Antonio-Alameda land transactions; the law practice of John Dwinelle; the law suits regarding the will of Josephine A. Phelps; the papers of Fanny J. Chipman, daughter of William Worthington Chipman; also a few mining papers (1862-1867).

Moreover, the collection contains the daily journal of William W. Chipman for 1861 and 1862 and his record of the details of the cases he handled between 1863 and 1867. The combination of these documents gives a rare glimpse into the legal practice of a nineteenth-century lawyer before state and federal courts.

Subject Headings:

Contracts
Corporations
Estates
Insurance
Law & Practice
Natural Resources
Real Property
Title

COUTS, CAVE JOHNSON (1821-1874)
approximately 16,000 pieces, 1832-1951

Cave J. Couts, an army officer sent to California in 1848, married the daughter of Juan Bandini and became the owner of the large Guajome Rancho in San Diego County. Couts attended the U.S. Military Academy from 1838 to 1843, was ordered to Monterey, Mexico, with the First Dragoons and then to California. In 1849 he led the escort for the U.S. Boundary Commission mapping the border from San Diego to the Colorado River. After his marriage in 1851, he engaged in the cattle business on his extensive rancho. His son, Cave J. Couts, Jr. (1865-1943), became a civil engineer and worked in Central America and as a deputy surveyor for San Diego County in 1884. Thereafter he managed the Guajome Ranch and engaged in various business ventures.

This is a significant collection. The land papers are very extensive and useful. The various estate papers are useful summaries of late nineteenth- and early twentieth-century economic practices. Other documents concern the history of San Diego County, particularly Indians (including the uprising led by Antonio Garra in 1851); ranchos and cities (with survey maps and land papers); Mission San Luis Rey; the cattle industry. Other legal topics concern negotiable instruments, natural resources, and family law.

Subject Headings:
Contracts
Estates
Family Law
Natural Resources
Real Property

CRANK, JAMES FILLMORE (1842-1928)
450 pieces, 1880-1902

James F. Crank came to California from New York in 1874 and bought the Fair Oaks Ranch in Pasadena from Benjamin S. Eaton in 1877. Crank was active in Los Angeles, where he organized the First National Bank, became an owner of the *Los Angeles Times*, helped secure Westlake Park for the city, and gave land for the Raymond Hotel in Pasadena. He was instrumental in the founding of the Los Angeles and San

Gabriel Valley Railroad, which began operation in 1885 and was sold to the Santa Fe Railroad in 1887. He built the first cable street railway in the West in Los Angeles in 1889 and helped found the city of Monrovia, California, in 1886.

This is a significant collection. Crank's letterbooks contain extensive correspondence involving municipal, railroad, and corporation law issues. The business papers of the Los Angeles Cable Railway and Pacific Railway Company in box 11 are useful. Other documents concern the development of Los Angeles County, particularly city and interurban railways (Los Angeles Cable Railway Co., Pacific Railway Co., Los Angeles and San Gabriel Valley Railroad Co., Los Angeles Development Co.); the wine industry (Sierra Madre Vintage Co., Lamanda Park, California); the Fair Oaks Ranch, Pasadena; and the Azusa Land and Water Co. Other topics of interest include bankruptcy, taxation, corporation, real estate, municipal, and contract.

Subject Headings:
Agriculture
Contracts
Corporations
Debtor & Creditor
Municipalities
Natural Resources
Railroads
Real Property
Taxation
Water

DALTON, HENRY (1804-1884)
2,430 pieces, 1819-1942

Henry Dalton, California land owner and businessman, was born in London and engaged in the coastal trade in Peru and Mexico before acquiring property in California in 1843. After his purchase of Rancho Azusa in 1844, Dalton eventually became the owner of five adjacent ranches. In 1847 he married Maria Guadalupe Zamorano, daughter of Agustin Vicente Zamorano. During the conflict between Mexico and the United States, Dalton supported the Mexican side and suffered damages and losses of livestock on his properties as a result of the war. After American occupation he lost much of his land to squatters and in litigation with the government. He spent the rest of his life trying to settle his claims against Mexico and the United States.

This is a significant collection. It provides a rare and comprehensive picture of the longevity and complexity of the struggles over Mexican private land grants in California. The collection is especially valuable in detailing the importance of the surveying aspects of those grants. The Dalton correspondence makes it abundantly clear that obtaining a patent of the most favorable survey (which were also litigated in the courts) was more time-consuming and fraught with legal battles than actually winning title in the first place.

Moreover, the collection reveals how grantees struggled with squatters, often coming to interesting accommodations with them. The collection documents Dalton's efforts to have his confirmed land grants re-surveyed from the mid-1860s through 1883. Boxes 5-10 trace this saga and contain extensive correspondence with his numerous lawyers. The Rancho Azusa water rights papers, 1866-1883, are in box 14.

Subject Headings:
Law & Practice
Real Property
Title
Water

DANE FAMILY COLLECTION
1,030 pieces, 1849-1934

Ezra Dane (1828-1921) crossed the plains to California in 1852 and engaged in mining in the Tuolomne region. He married in 1859, established a home in Sonora, California, and in 1884 acquired a fruit ranch, "Sunny Ridge," near Pasadena, California. George Ezra Dane (1904-1941), grandson of Ezra Dane, was a lawyer and a writer of folklore, western history, and humor.

This collection is moderately significant because it contains a "lawyer's diary" with observations of Sacramento and San Francisco, 1854-1857 (Box 1). The diary topics include crime and law practice.

Subject Headings:
Crimes
Law & Practice
Real Property

EL DORADO COUNTY ARCHIVES
approximately 1,600 pieces, 1850-1906

El Dorado County, California, in the Sierra Nevada east of Sacramento in the heart of the gold mining country, was established in 1850 with Placerville as the county seat.

This is a significant collection of nineteenth-century court records. The documents concern El Dorado County government and administration, as seen in court records (justice court records, 1862-1886, and county court records, (1852-1869); land records (1871-1892); school records (1867-1880); treasury records, including tax rolls (1852-1869), assessment rolls (1852-1869), etc.; merchandising accounts, principally for mining camps (1855-1900); mining papers and records (time books, claim books), many from the El Dorado Water and Deep Gravel Mining Co. (1855-1883).

Subject Headings:
Commercial Law
Law & Practice
Natural Resources
Real Property
Taxation

FERNALD, CHARLES (1830-1892)
8,160 pieces, 1852-1904

Charles Fernald, pioneer Santa Barbara (California) jurist, came to California in 1848, tried mining in the Mother Lode, then went in 1850 to San Francisco, where he became a self-taught lawyer and a member of the California Bar at the age of twenty-two. Fernald settled in Santa Barbara and was elected, successively, sheriff, district attorney, and judge of Santa Barbara County, and became recognized as a leading authority on Mexican land grants.

This is a significant collection. The land papers in the collection are substantial in number and the correspondence with Thomas Bard provides insight into the development of Union Oil of California. Numerous documents reveal a great deal about law practice in nineteenth-century California. Other topics include real property (mortgage), railroad, taxation, estate, constitutional, landlord and tenant, and debtor and creditor.

Subject Headings:
Admiralty
Commercial Law
Constitutional Law
Contracts
Corporations
Crimes
Debtor & Creditor
Estates
Landlord & Tenant
Law & Practice
Municipalities
Natural Resources
Railroads
Real Property
Taxation
Torts
Water

FORD, JOHN ANSON (1883-1983)
approximately 35,000 pieces, 1832-1971

John Anson Ford was a member of the Los Angeles County Board of Supervisors from 1934 to 1958 and served as chairman from 1952 to 1954 and in 1957. He attended Beloit College in Wisconsin, taught history and economics, then became a news writer for the Chicago *Tribune* and for the Department of Labor and Agriculture in Washington, D.C. Ford came to Los Angeles in 1920 and entered the public relations business. In 1937, after his election as Los Angeles County supervisor, he was chosen by the Recall Committee as candidate for mayor of Los Angeles but worked instead for the election of Fletcher Bowron (q.v.). Ford retired from the Board of Supervisors in 1958, but continued to write newspaper columns and to serve the community.

This is a moderately significant collection containing extensive documents on oil, water, crime, taxation, and municipal matters. Documents concern primarily Los Angeles County government in the fields of agriculture, education, finance, labor, law enforcement, minority groups, music and art, politics, recreation, and welfare.

Subject Headings:
Crimes
Environmental Law
Municipalities
Natural Resources
Taxation
Water

GRAVES, JACKSON ALPHEUS (1852-1933)
approximately 14,000 pieces, 1878-1930

Jackson A. Graves, pioneer Los Angeles lawyer and businessman, was born in Iowa and came to California in 1857. He graduated from St. Mary's College in San Francisco in 1872 and studied law in the firm of Eastman and Neumann. Graves moved to Los Angeles in 1875. In 1888, after membership in various partnerships, Graves joined Henry O'Melveny, and the firm became Graves, O'Melveny and Shankland until its dissolution in 1904. Graves was vice-president of Farmers and Merchants National Bank in 1903 and president from 1920-1933.

This is a significant collection. The letterbooks, letters, and documents in this collection span the period 1878-1930 and involve the critical issues of legal practice: land titles, contracts, mortgages, debtor/creditor relations, and corporations. For students of legal history, this collection is quite valuable. Other correspondence concerns banking and finance, seen chiefly in the business correspondence of Jackson A. Graves mainly with Isaias W. Hellman, Sr., president of the Farmers and Merchants Bank (Los Angeles) from 1875 to 1920 and president of Wells Fargo Nevada National Bank in San Francisco from 1890 to 1920; also land papers of the Los Angeles area and papers of California law firms. Other topics on the collection include agriculture (citrus business), taxation, estate, water, municipal, natural resources (oil), crime, insurance, landlord and tenant, and lawyers.

Subject Headings:

Admiralty
Agriculture
Banking
Commercial Law
Contracts
Corporations
Crimes
Debtor & Creditor
Estates
Insurance
Landlord & Tenant
Law & Practice
Municipalities
Natural Recources

Public Utilities
Railroads
Taxation
Torts
Water

HAIGHT, HENRY HUNTLEY (1825-1878)
508 pieces, 1846-1865

Henry H. Haight, California governor, was born in New York and graduated from Yale University in 1844. He was admitted to the bar in St. Louis, Missouri, where he practiced law until 1850. He then traveled to California and settled in San Francisco. Haight practiced law there until 1867 when as candidate of the Democratic party, he was elected governor of California. During his term of office he led the fight against railroad subsidies. The University of California was established (1868) during this period also. After losing his bid for reelection in 1871, Haight returned to private practice until his death.

This is a moderately significant collection. Documents on law practice in the 1850s and debtor/creditor relations are most useful. Other topics include real property and bankruptcy.

In particular, the collection sheds much light on the nature and validity of land titles to property in San Francisco during the 1850s and 1860s.

Subject Headings:
Admiralty
Commercial Law
Constitutional Law
Contracts
Corporations
Crimes
Debtor & Creditor
Estates

Family Law
Law & Practice
Natural Resources
Railroads
Real Property
Taxation
Title

HALLECK, PEACHY & BILLINGS (firm)
80 pieces, 1837-1861

Halleck, Peachy & Billings was one of the most prestigious law firms on the Pacific Coast. Its headquarters were in San Francisco and it specialized in California land cases. The firm was organized by Frederick Billings and Alexander Carey Peachy in 1849 and they were soon joined by Henry Wager Halleck. Halleck, (1815-1872) was a West Point graduate sent to California at the beginning of the Mexican War. He served as secretary of state under military governors of California and helped frame the California Constitution. He wrote the report on land titles used to formulate the Land Act of 1851, which required all claimants to Mexican land grants to seek confirmation of their titles before a special federal land board. Halleck became active in the firm of Halleck, Peachy & Billings and resigned from the army in 1854. Archibald Carey Peachy (1820-1883) was a native of Virginia who came to California in 1849 and joined Billings in forming the law firm. He was elected to the state assembly in 1852 and to the senate in 1860. Frederick Billings (1823-1890) graduated from the University of Vermont in 1844, was admitted to the bar in 1849, and was appointed legal advisor to California territory under Governor Mason. The firm was dissolved in 1861 with the coming of the Civil War, and Halleck returned to the army, where he served as general-in-chief (1862-1864) and as an aide to Abraham Lincoln. Frederick Billings returned to

Vermont after the war and later became president of the Northern Pacific Railroad.

This is a significant collection particularly for the land papers. The collection also contains documents on admiralty cases. Despite the few documents in the collection, the materials are rich in legal history and should be read with the Halleck, Peachy & Billings papers held at the Bancroft Library. Other documents in the collection concern California land cases—copies of land titles, drafts of briefs, and opinions used in establishing the legal titles of some thirty-six different land grants. The collection includes notes on Spanish land law and a few papers relating to other legal cases in California.

Subject Headings:
Admiralty
Debtor & Creditor
Law & Practice
Real Property
Title

HESLOP FAMILY COLLECTION
40 pieces, 1833-1858; 1880-1906

Members of the Heslop family were pioneer landowners in East Pasadena, California. Jose Heslop (1835) was born of English and Chilean parents in Valparaiso, Chile, and came to California where he married Francisca White. She was the daughter of Michael White, an English sailor who came early to California and married the daughter of Eulalia Perez de Guillen, through whom Francisca inherited portions of Rancho San Pascual (now Pasadena) and Rancho Muscupiabe near San Bernardino.

This collection is of marginal significance, but does contain various land papers including land dealings near the city of Pasadena and the litigation for the title of Rancho Muscupiabe.

Subject Headings:
Contracts
Real Property
Water

HOADLEY, MILO (1809-1887)
65 pieces, 1849-1886

Milo Hoadley, civil engineer, came to San Francisco, California, from Connecticut in 1849. He served as assistant and deputy county surveyor and was elected state surveyor general in 1851. Hoadley was involved in negotiations for the water supply for the city of San Francisco, served as president of the San Francisco City Board of Civil Engineers (1862-1863), and later practiced privately as a civil engineer.

This collection is moderately significant. Hoadley's correspondence on water is useful as are his field notes on San Francisco's water supply needs. Hoadley's journal in box 2 is for the period 1850-1852 and contains observations on the 1851 San Francisco Vigilance Committee. Other documents concern life in and near San Francisco (1850-1852), official and private surveys made in San Francisco city and county (1849-1862), and land titles in San Francisco city and county; information on the controversy in supplying water to San Francisco (1852-1872), in which Hoadley's San Francisco Water Co., organized in 1867, unsuccessfully tried to displace the monopolist Spring Valley Co.

Subject Headings:
Crimes
Natural Resources
Real Property
Water

HOUGHTON, SHERMAN OTIS (1828-1914)
195 pieces, 1831-1914

Sherman O. Houghton, California lawyer and politician, was born in New York and came to California with Stevenson's New York Volunteers in 1847. In 1849 he settled in San Jose where he became mayor in 1853. Houghton was admitted to the bar in 1857 and used his knowledge of Spanish to specialize in land claims cases brought about by the transfer from Mexican to American jurisdiction. In 1861 he married Eliza Poor Donner, whose parents, George and Tamsen Donner, had perished during the crossing of the Sierra Nevada in 1846. Houghton served in the U.S. House of Representatives from 1871 to 1875. In 1900 he retired to a ranch in Los Angeles County.

This collection is of marginal significance. The collection contains some land papers, including an abstract of title for a portion of Rancho Azusa (1885). Other topics in the collection involve family law and contract.

Subject Headings:
Contracts
Family Law
Landlord & Tenant
Real Property

HOWELL (EVELYN LIONEL VICTOR) COLLECTION
70 pieces, 1831-1905

This collection consists of various legal papers relating to land in California, collected by Evelyn L. V. Howell, weather station observer at Mission San Juan Capistrano. Included are land patents, indentures, mortgages and deeds, principally from Los Angeles and San Diego Counties and in the vicinity of San Juan Capistrano.

This collection is of marginal significance, containing assorted land papers and some landlord and tenant materials.

Subject Headings:
Landlord & Tenant
Real Property

JACKS, DAVID (1822-1909)
approximately 200,000 pieces, ca.1845-1926

David Jacks, pioneeer businessman in Monterey, California, came to New York from Scotland in 1841, and sailed around the Horn to California in 1848. In 1850 he settled in Monterey, where he acquired extensive land holdings and became a farmer and stock raiser. Jacks was involved in much litigation concerning his properties, including a suit by the city of Monterey in 1877 to regain land held by Jacks. He was instrumental in the construction of the Monterey and Salinas Valley Railroad in 1874, in establishing the Pacific Grove Retreat, and in the funding of the city of Del Monte.

This is a significant collection. The land papers are extensive as is the litigation over title to land. Jacks' correspondence with his numerous lawyers spans the late nineteenth century and the issues of the day: land title, contract, landlord and tenant, and creditor/debtor relations. Jacks had his own law library and frequently debated "law" with his lawyers.

Subject Headings:
Agriculture
Crimes
Landlord & Tenant
Law & Practice
Railroads
Real Property
Title

JONES, ELBERT P. (ca.1823-1852)
approximately 100 pieces, 1830; 1848-1914

Dr. Elbert P. Jones, early San Francisco lawyer, was a native of Kentucky who came to California in 1847. He was the first editor of the *California Star* and was elected to the San Francisco town council in 1847. Jones became the proprietor of Portsmouth House in San Francisco and was a prominent investor in real estate in the city.

This collection is of marginal significance. The land papers for San Francisco are of general form. Other documents concern the claim of Jones' heirs, particularly Mrs. Anna M. R. Jones of Westchester, Pennsylvania, to Yerba Buena Island, California, ca.1901-1914; also includes records of transfer and diagrams of lots of land in San Francisco sold by Elbert P. Jones, 1848-1851.

Subject Headings:
Commercial Law
Estates
Law & Practice
Real Property
Title

KELLER, MATTHEW (1810-1881)
365 pieces, 1851-1959

Matthew Keller, Los Angeles pioneer businessman and ranch owner, was born in Ireland and graduated from Trinity College, Dublin. In 1832 he went to New York, migrated to Texas in the mid-1830s and spent the next twelve to fifteen years in Mexico. Keller returned to the United States, first to New Orleans, and then to San Francisco (in 1849) before settling in Los Angeles in 1851. He opened a general merchandise store and purchased property on Alameda and Aliso Streets, where he built his home, planted fruit trees and vineyards, and established the Rising Sun and Los Angeles Vineyards

Winery. He experimented with horticulture, held several public offices, was a director of the Pioneer Oil Company, and became the owner of many pieces of property in Los Angeles, vineyards in Anaheim, and the thirteen-thousand acre Rancho Malibu. His son, Henry Workman Keller, was a director of the Automobile Club of Southern California and was active in the promotion of the Pan American Highway, for which he was honored by the Mexican government.

This is a moderately significant collection, particularly the land papers. Documents generally concern early Los Angeles after 1850 as seen in the correspondence and land papers of Matthew Keller, expecially concerning the wine industry (Rising Sun and Los Angeles Vineyards Winery). Other legal topics are negotiable instruments, contract, and natural resources.

Subject Headings:
Agriculture
Commercial Law
Contracts
Corporations
Estates
Landlord & Tenant
Natural Resources
Real Property
Title
Water

KINKADE, JOHN THOMPSON (1828-1904)
91 pieces, 1829-1885

John T. Kinkade, California lawyer, was born in Virginia and attended Bethany College. He then traveled in the midwest with his uncle and guardian, E. Kinkade. Afterward, John T. Kinkade graduated from Wesleyan University in 1844, then returned to Virginia where he was admitted to the bar in 1848. The following year he crossed the plains to California.

He engaged in mining along the American River in Placer County until 1869, returning in 1870 to the practice of law in a small mining town, and then in Auburn. Kinkade was active in Republican politics and served as Placer County superintendent of schools for six years.

This collection is of marginal significance, although several letters concerning water are of interest and Kinkade's 1856 letter to James Kinkade contains comments on the 1856 San Francisco Vigilance Committee (box 2, indexed under crime).

Subject Headings:
Crimes
Natural Resources
Water

LEIDESDORFF, WILLIAM ALEXANDER (1810-1848)
502 pieces, 1840-1867

William A. Leidesdorff, early California trader and official, was born in the Danish West Indies of a Danish father and mulatto mother. In 1841 he came to California as master of the ship "Julia Ann." He engaged in trade between Hawaii and San Francisco, and afterwards began a general exporting business in San Francisco. Leidesdorff became a Mexican citizen in 1844 and received a grant for Rancho Rio de los Americanos, east of Fort Sutter. The next year he was appointed vice-consul of the United States, and remained prominent in the affairs of San Francisco until his death in 1848.

This is a moderately significant collection. The correspondence covers a broad range of subjects concerning contracts, commerce, and real estate. Other documents are letters, mostly received by Leidesdorff in the 1840s, concerning coastal trade and life in the mercantile business in San Francisco. The collection includes considerable correspondence with Thomas O. Larkin, John A. Sutter, and other prominent Californians, as well as with the Russian American Fur Company. Much of the correspondence deals with disputes and dealings in San Francisco lands, including the Peter Smith deeds, water lots, the Bolton and Barron claim, and the Ritchie claim for Rancho Suisun. Moreover, the correspondence contains observations on the operation of the Board of Land Commissioners and various speculative schemes to obtain San Francisco property. Other legal topics include negotiable instruments and law practice.

Subject Headings:
Admiralty
Commercial Law
Contracts
Crimes
Estates
Landlord & Tenant
Law & Practice
Real Property
Title

McCULLOUGH, SAMUEL (1826-ca.1890)
72 pieces, 1854-1886

Samuel McCullough, California businessman and state assemblyman, came in 1855 from New Jersey to Sacramento, California, where he practiced his trade as a carpenter. In 1858 he joined the gold rush to the Fraser River in Canada, but in 1860 returned to San Francisco where he worked as a building contractor and hotel proprietor. McCullough served in the California state assembly from 1871 to 1873, and was superintendent of U.S. Government buildings in San Francisco from 1873 to 1878.

This collection is of marginal significance. The letterbook contains some useful materials on contracts and an 1858 letter to Caroline Rush is of interest for Sacramento land titles. Other documents are personal and business papers, mostly relating to the construction of federal buildings in San

Francisco from 1873-1878, the Sutter New Helvetia title, and a trip to the Fraser River mines.

Subject Headings:
Contracts
Estates
Real Property
Title

MANDEVILLE, JAMES WYLIE (1824-1876)
approximately 725 pieces, 1848-1866

James W. Mandeville, California politician and surveyor, was a schoolteacher in his native New York before coming to San Jose, California, in 1849. A year later, he left teaching there to engage in mining in Tuolomne County. He was elected to serve in the state assembly from 1853 to 1854 and in the state senate from 1855 to 1857. Mandeville became U.S. surveyor from 1857 to 1861, and afterwards held the offices of state commissioner of immigration and state controller in 1875.

This is a moderately significant collection. Mandeville's correspondence ranges over a wide range of legal subjects concentrated in the period 1851-1857. Topics include natural resources (mining), water, constitutional (sabbath), municipal, taxation, and crime. State and local political issues frequently emerge from the letters, including the Broderick-Gwin rivalry of 1855-1857.

Subject Headings:
Constitutional Law
Contracts
Crimes
Debtor & Creditor
Municipalities
Natural Resources
Real Property
Taxation
Water

MARKHAM, HENRY HARRISON (1840-1923)
approximately 2,494 pieces, 1867-1899

Henry H. Markham, governor of California, was born in New York and was educated at Wheeler's Academy in Vermont. He served in the Civil War, and afterward studied law in Wisconsin. Markham practiced law in Wisconsin until 1879, when he moved to California, settled in Pasadena, and became a prominent and influential citizen. His business enterprises were varied, but his chief interests were in gold and silver mining in Arizona and California. Markham was elected a representative to Congress in 1884 and governor of California in 1890, which office he held until 1895.

This is a moderately significant collection containing land papers and correspondence on a wide variety of legal topics. Mining papers range from acquisition issues to tort. Other topics include water, corporation, railroad, constitutional, municipal, taxation, debtor and creditor, insurance, and courts.

Subject Headings:
Admiralty
Agriculture
Commercial Law
Constitutional Law
Contracts
Corporations
Debtor & Creditor
Estates
Insurance
Labor
Landlord & Tenant
Law & Practice
Municipalities
Natural Resources
Railroads

Real Property
Title
Water

MORGAN, WILLIAM R. (ca.1832-1901)
187 pieces, 1852-1886

William R. Morgan came to California from Bennington, Vermont, in 1852 to seek his fortune in the mines, and later became a state legislator. He settled in St. Louis, Sierra County, California, where he engaged in mining activities, eventually becoming secretary of the Sierra Union Water and Mining Company. Morgan served as state assemblyman from Sierra county in 1873 and 1874.

This is a moderately significant collection. Correspondence concerning the use of water for hydraulic mining is of particular legal significance. Other topics included in the collection are debtor and creditor, contract, mortgage, and real property.

Subject Headings:
Contracts
Corporations
Crimes
Debtor & Creditor
Landlord & Tenant
Natural Resources
Real Property
Taxation
Water

NEW ALMADEN MINE
45 pieces, 1853-1886

The New Almaden Mine, the mercury mine in Santa Clara

County, California, named for the Almaden Mine in Spain, ranked behind it as third richest in the world in extent and quality. For forty-five years the New Almaden produced an almost constant yield. The mine was visited in 1846 by Andres Castillero, an engineer and representative of the Mexican government, who formed the New Almaden Company, composed of several part-owners. An official survey of the property was not made until after the Civil War, and title to it had passed through several hands when the New Almaden Company brought its petition before the U.S. Land Commission in 1852. Litigation continued for twelve years, eventually reaching the U.S. Supreme Court. In 1857 the firm of Halleck, Peachy and Billings defended the New Almaden Mine Company against U.S. government charges that Castillero's claims were fraudulent. Government counsel Edmund Randolph's success helped bring about the verdict finally given in favor of the government in 1864, in a case in which even President Abraham Lincoln had at one time intervened. Although the claims of the Quicksilver Mining Company of New York, which had acquired partial title to the mine, were being upheld by the ruling in favor of the government, public opinion forced the New York company to purchase the assets of the New Almaden Company. The Quicksilver Mining Company continued to operate the mine successfully until 1890, followed by a period of gradual decline and bankruptcy in 1912.

This is a marginally significant collection. The item of greatest interest in this single box collection is a law firm notebook. It contains notes on title litigation and newspaper clippings providing a glimpse of law practice, 1858-1862. Other documents concern operation and business affairs of the New Almaden Mine, including legal documents (some concerning the land ownership case), reports on production and business accounts of the New Almaden Mine (1868-1886), reports to directors of the Quicksilver Mining Company (1868-1886), and correspondence relating to the mine.

Subject Headings:
Debtor & Creditor
Estates

Natural Resources
Real Property
Title

O'FARRELL, JASPER (1817-1875)
76 pieces, ca.1845-1924

Jasper O'Farrell, pioneer California politician and surveyor, was born in Ireland, where he received an education in civil engineering. In 1841 he joined a surveying expedition to South America and spent a year in Chile before his arrival in San Francisco in 1843. O'Farrell was employed as a surveyor by the Mexican authorities from 1844 to 1846, continued in government service under American rule, and made an official survey of San Francisco in 1847. He later engaged in mining on the Yuba River and in farming, ranching, and surveying in Sonoma County. He was active in politics, and was elected state senator from Sonoma and Mendocino Counties. O'Farrell died in San Francisco at the age of fifty-eight.

This collection is of marginal significance except for land papers in box 1. Documents concern personal, business, and political matters (1846-1875); rough survey notes and a few sketch maps of California ranchos and towns (ca.1845-ca.1850); and land papers pertaining to O'Farrell's property in Sonoma County (1855-1870).

Subject Headings:
Contracts
Landlord & Tenant
Real Property
Title

ORANGE COUNTY (CALIFORNIA) LAND PAPERS
approximately 1,200 pieces, 1887-1915

Orange County, California, was created in 1889 from part of Los Angeles County, and was named for the orange groves which were a predominant agricultural feature of the area. The county seat is Santa Ana. The earliest settlement in the county was at Mission San Juan Capristrano in 1776, and much of the land in Orange County, acquired by Spanish and Mexican grants, changed hands frequently. The predecessors of the Orange County Title Company, consolidated in 1894, transcribed the complete record of all Los Angeles County documents pertaining to Orange County land titles at the time of the county's creation.

This collection is of marginal significance. The materials involved land title transfers for the period 1885-1915 and are of a general form.

Subject Heading:
Real Property

PARK, ALICE LOCKE (1861-ca.1950)
795 pieces, 1898-1953

Alice Locke Park, feminist, reformer, and pacifist, was born in Boston in 1861 but lived most of her life in California. She was active in both national and international organizations for the improvement of prison conditions, labor laws, humane education, wild life conservation, and the preservation of natural resources. Her primary interest, however, was in women's rights and she was assistant director of the Susan B. Anthony Memorial Committee. She wrote and promoted the California law, adopted in 1913, granting to women equal rights of guardianship over their children.

This significant collection contains substantial correspondence about women's suffrage, women's legal rights, and women's issues. The suffrage documents concern the California campaign as well as the national constitutional amendment movement. Further, a good deal of correspondence addresses birth control, community property, and divorce law. Other topics include crime and family law.

Subject Headings:
Constitutional Law
Crimes
Family Law
Labor

POTTER, CHARLES F. AND ISAAC B.
approximately 5,000 pieces, 1905-1940

Charles F. Potter and his brother, Isaac B. Potter, were lawyers with offices in Los Angeles and San Francisco. Their clients were chiefly water and power companies in the southwestern United States. Charles Potter was a director of the Mono Power Company in 1920.

This is a significant collection, particularly for insights on irrigation and hydroelectric power. The collection contains extensive correspondence with the Cain Irrigation Company, the California-Nevada Canal, Water and Power Company, the Central California Electric Company, the Hillsdale Water Company, the Mono Power Company, Pacific Power Company, the Sierras Construction Company, the Southern Sierras Power Company, Bishop Light and Power Company, and materials on the Fish Slough Project in Mono and Inyo counties. Water law issues as well as land papers are to be found in most of the collection's boxes. Other topics include mortgage, public utility, and contract.

Subject Headings:
Contracts
Corporations
Landlord & Tenant
Natural Resources
Public Utilities
Real Property
Title
Water

PRICE, RODMAN McCAMLEY (1816-1894)
156 pieces, 1842-ca.1890

Rodman McCamley Price, naval officer, governor of New Jersey, and businessman, was born in New York, attended the College of New Jersey, and studied law. He was appointed a naval purser in 1840, serving first on the frigates "Fulton" and "Missouri." In 1846 he was sent to California aboard the ship "Cyane," landing in Monterey with the American occupation forces. He served as alcalde of Monterey, was a member of San Francisco's first municipal council, and of the first California Constitutional Convention in 1849. Price invested heavily in San Francisco real estate. He returned to New Jersey in 1850, and with his partner, Samuel Ward, established the New York office of Ward & Price, Bankers and Agents for California. In New Jersey he served as congressman (1851-1853) and governor (1854-1857), and helped establish the state's public school system.

This collection is of marginal significance except for the land papers in box 1 that include news of the business affairs of the firm of Ward & Price and of San Francisco property values and land titles.

Subject Headings:
Landlord & Tenant
Title

RAILROADIANA (WESTERN U.S.A.)
41 pieces, 1860-1879

The collection of Railroadiana is composed of material concerning the Central Pacific and the Southern Pacific Railroads and the smaller lines (the California Pacific, the California Pacific Extension, the Northern, and the Western Pacific railroad companies) eventually acquired by the two larger railroads. The owners of the Central Pacific, which was completed as a cross-country route in 1869, had chartered the

Southern Pacific Railroad Company in 1865. Through acquisition of smaller branch lines, the construction of several new ones, and the consolidation of their enterprises, the "Big Four," Collis P. Huntington, Leland Stanford, Mark Hopkins, and Charles Crocker, created a vast transportation monopoly, serving a large portion of the western United States. Alfred Andrew Cohen (1829-1887), a lawyer who figures prominently in this collection sold his interests in several smaller California railroads to the Central Pacific Railroad in 1869. He served as an attorney for the Central Pacific, but resigned in 1876 in protest against the railroad policies. The companies brought litigation against him in retaliation for his efforts to introduce legislation to regulate railroad fares and rates in California. Eventually cordial relations were once more restored and the influential lawyer again defended the interests of Central Pacific.

This collection is of marginal significance, except for the transcript of the Central Pacific Railroad Company v. Alfred A. Cohen case (1876).

Subject Headings:
Railroads

RUSSELL, MAJORS & WADDELL
508 pieces, 1839-1868

The firm of Russell, Majors & Waddell, freighters, stagecoach operators, and originators of the Pony Express, was established in 1854. The principals of the company, William Hepburn Russell (1828-1872), William Bradford Waddell (1807-1872), and Alexander Majors (1814-1900), had been active in many business ventures together before consolidating their firm. All three had been involved in retailing. Russell and Majors were in the Santa Fe trade and Waddell had helped organize small railroads. The company received a government contract to supply the Army of Utah, a force sent to suppress Mormon rebellion. In 1859 they organized the

Leavenworth & Pike's Peak Express Company, which, in 1860, became the Central Overland California & Pike's Peak Express Company, chartered to carry mail from St. Louis, Missouri, to San Francisco. In 1860, urged chiefly by Russell, the company began operation of the Pony Express, which carried mail by the central route for eighteen months until its demise was brought on by the completion of a transcontinental telegraph service. The firm of Russell, Majors & Waddell collapsed in 1861, following a financial scandal, and declared bankruptcy. After the partners surrendered their personal fortunes, the company was purchased at auction by Ben Holladay in 1862.

This collection has minimal significance for legal history. The topics of interest in the collection include contract and debtor and creditor. Other documents involve the business and legal papers of Russell, Majors & Waddell, freighting operations, the mercantile business, land transactions, and the Pony Express.

Subject Headings:
Contracts
Debtor & Creditor

SAN FRANCISCO COMMITTEE OF VIGILANCE, 1856

approximately 3,750 pieces, 1853-1858

The San Francisco Committees of Vigilance of 1851 and 1856 were formed when crime became widespread in the city of San Francisco in the wake of the Gold Rush. The city was without adequate processes of law, and the courts were a public scandal. As a means to preserve social order, a vigilance committee was formed for the administration of summary justice. The original committee, organized in the spring of 1851, disbanded after four months of vigorous activity served to accomplish its purpose. The reform was not a lasting one, however, and in 1856 renewed abuses by corrupt officials brought about a revival of the movement on a greatly augmented scale. The murder of James King of William sparked the reactivation of vigilante activity. King, a crusading San Francisco newspaper editor, was shot by James P. Casey, a corrupt official, after King attacked Casey in the columns of his paper. Immediately ten thousand men hastened to join the vigilantes, including many veterans of the earlier committee. William T. Coleman was again chosen as leader, and the members were organized into companies and regiments. Opposition to the vigilance committee was led by California Supreme Court Justice David S. Terry, but the efforts of his group were largely ineffective. The "Great Committee" of the vigilantes functioned for five months, then surrendered its powers to a regularly constituted civil authority.

This is a significant collection. No student of vigilance in the west can study the subject without reference to this collection. The documents include individuals making charges or giving information about suspects or prisoners to the San Francisco Committee of Vigilance of 1856, applications for membership, lists of members and members of the executive committee, and financial documents.

Subject Heading:
Crimes

SHORB, JAMES de BARTH (1842-1896)
approximately 10,600 pieces, 1816-1931

James de Barth Shorb, an attorney and civil engineer from Maryland, came to California in 1864 to represent the Philadelphia and California Petroleum Company. He was later an engineer with the United States Army. After his marriage to Maria de Jesus Wilson in 1867, Shorb joined his father-in-law, Benjamin Davis Wilson, in the development of their extensive land holdings and in the founding of the San Gabriel Winery. Shorb constructed and was president of the San Gabriel Valley Railroad and the Alhambra Railroad. He was active in many business ventures and served as Los Angeles County treasurer in 1892.

This is a significant collection involving the lives and transactions of some of the most influential people in southern California. The legal materials generated by the vast land and citrus business deserve close scholarly scrutiny. Documents concern personal and business affairs of James de Barth Shorb; the San Marino Ranch (now the city of San Marino, California), land development in Southern California, the citrus and wine industries in California (especially the San Gabriel Winery owned by Benjamin Davis Wilson and managed by James de Barth Shorb), and California politics.

Subject Headings:
Agriculture
Commercial Law
Constitutional Law
Contracts
Corporations
Debtor & Creditor
Environmental Law
Estates
Labor
Landlord & Tenant
Law & Practice
Natural Resources
Patent
Railroads
Real Property
Taxation
Torts
Water

STANTON, PHILIP ACKLEY (1868-1945)
approximately 265 pieces, 1909-1929

Philip A. Stanton, Los Angeles realtor and California politician, was born and educated in Ohio. He came to California in 1887, became president of several real estate companies, and was responsible for building the towns of Huntington Beach, Seal Beach, and Stanton. He served in the California assembly (1903-1909), as candidate for governor of California in the primary election of 1910, and as a member of the Republican National Committee for California (1912-1916).

This is a marginally significant collection. Topics included in the collection are insurance, constitutional, and estate.

Subject Headings:
Constitutional Law
Estates
Insurance

STEARNS, ABEL (1798-1871)
approximately 12,500 pieces, 1821-1935

Abel Stearns, pioneer ranch owner and businessman of Los Angeles, left Massachusetts as a young man to engage in the South American and China shipping trade. He went to Mexico in 1826, became a naturalized citizen, and in 1828 moved to Monterey, California, where he went into merchandising. In about 1833 Stearns settled in Los Angeles, joined Juan Bandini in the trading business, and married Bandini's daughter Arcadia. Stearns became involved in almost every type of business, held minor political offices, and was sent as a representative of the Los Angeles district to the state constitutional convention in Monterey in 1849. He began acquiring rancho property and by 1858 was the owner of vast land holdings and cattle herds and the wealthiest man in Los Angeles county. As a member of the state assembly in 1861, he took an active part in promoting the Los Angeles and San Pedro Railroad. Stearns was forced to sell a great deal of his property when he became bankrupt after the drought of 1863-1864, which caused the decline of the cattle industry in California. He died in San Francisco in 1871.

This is a significant collection containing extensive land papers and correspondence. Stearns' affairs were various and his letters demonstrate the boundless reach of his enterprises. Documents concern life in California during the Mexican and early statehood periods, with cattle raising, trading transactions (especially in hides and tallow), ranchos of Upper and Lower California, land titles and transfers, political and social life, and the gold discoveries in Southern California in 1842. Also included are diaries written in the Santa Monica area (1879-1905) by Juan Bautista Bandini, son of Juan Bandini. There is a small sub-collection, the Gaffey Papers, assembled by John Tracy Gaffey, who married Arcadia Bandini, niece of Mrs. Abel Stearns. They consist of correspondence, including letters from Stephen Mallory White, papers relating to San Pedro, California, and historical sketches. White was an attorney and U.S. Senator. Other legal topics include taxation.

Subject Headings:
Commercial Law
Real Property
Taxation
Title

STIMSON, MARSHALL (1876-1951)
932 pieces, 1893-1951

Marshall Stimson, Los Angeles lawyer, came to Pasadena, California, from Massachusetts with his family in 1887, but returned to Harvard College, where he graduated in 1901, and began to practice law in Boston. In 1903 Stimson moved his practice to Los Angeles, where he became an important figure in civic affairs. He was instrumental in the development of Los Angeles Harbor, director of the Los Angeles Chamber of Commerce, and active in reform movements in state and local governments. Stimson was prominent in Republican politics, and organized the Lincoln-Roosevelt

Republican League of California (1907) and the Progressive Party in California (1912). He was also active in supporting the League of Nations and the United Nations.

This is a marginally significant collection. Documents include radio addresses of Marshall Stimson, and the manuscript of his autobiography; California and national politics (including Hiram Johnson and the Progressive Party "Bull Moose" Convention of 1912), General Homer Lea, the League of Nations, and World War II.

Subject Headings:
Commercial Law
Estates
Law & Practice
Natural Resources
Real Property
Taxation

TERRY, DAVID SMITH (1823-1889)
260 pieces, 1849-1933

David Smith Terry, lawyer, politician, and California Supreme Court justice, was born in Kentucky and lived in Texas during the Revolution. Terry began the practice of law in Texas in 1845, joined the Texas Rangers during the Mexican War, then went to California to seek gold in 1849. He returned to Texas to marry Cornelia Runnels in 1852, then settled in California, where he became active in politics and was elected a judge of the Supreme Court in 1855. Political rivalry with David C. Broderick, U.S. Senator from California, culminated in the famous Terry-Broderick duel in 1859, in which Broderick was killed. Terry joined the Confederate army during the Civil War, returning afterward to California to resume his law practice. He met his death following the famous Hill-Sharon divorce case when he was shot after a personal feud with Justice Stephen J. Field.

This is a moderately significant collection on two grounds. Terry's correspondence with his wife contains observations on the 1856 San Francisco Vigilance Committee. Second, Terry's letters address problems of frontier law practice, most importantly, his felt need to seek "rapid fortunes at the law." His observations about the costs of mining litigation in Nevada where he sought his fortune are particularly worthwhile although not part of California legal history. Other topics of interest include crime, real property (mortgage), and taxation.

Subject Headings:
Crimes
Debtor & Creditor
Law & Practice
Real Property
Taxation

WATKINS, LOUISE (WARD) (1890-1974)
approximately 7,500 pieces 1871-1974

Louise Whipple (Ward) Watkins, leader in women's rights, California politics, and Los Angeles organizations, came to California from New York with her family when she was fifteen years old. Her father, George Clinton Ward, was a prominent civil engineer and became president of the Southern California Edison Company. Louise Ward studied dramatics in New York and law at the University of Southern California. In 1915 she married Edward Francis Watkins, the son of Edward Lancaster Watkins, early Southern California pioneer. Mrs. Watkins was active in the cause of woman suffrage, women's clubs, the Japan American Society, and Republican politics. She served on several state commissions, founded the Southern California Republican Women (1935), and ran for the U.S. Senate in 1938.

This is a marginally significant collection. For social, political, and family history, it contains a wealth of material.

The family correspondence is voluminous and spans generations as well as a century of time. The correspondence of Louise Watkins with her mother in 1947 and with a variety of individuals in 1952 contains interesting material on family law. Other topics of interest in the collection include crime and debtor and creditor.

Subject Headings:
Crimes
Debtor & Creditor
Family Law
Labor
Taxation

WILSON, BENJAMIN DAVIS (1811-1878)
approximately 3,500 pieces, 1847-1920

Benjamin D. Wilson, pioneer California rancher and businessman, was a native of Tennessee who came to California from New Mexico in 1841 as a member of the Rowland-Workman party. He bought the Jurupa Rancho (Riverside, California) in 1843 and in 1844 married Ramona Yorba, daughter of Bernardo Yorba, well-known land owner during the Mexican period. After Ramona's death, Wilson in 1853 married Margaret S. Hereford, a widow from St. Louis related to the Sublette family of the Rocky Mountain Fur Company. She had gone with her husband to Santa Fe, then to Chihuahua, Mexico, making her way to California by steamer via Mazatlan, while her husband (who died a year later) came overland. Wilson became prominent as California changed from Mexican to American rule. In 1851-1852, he was elected the second mayor of Los Angeles, in 1852 he served as U.S. Indian Agent under Superintendent Edward F. Beale, and in 1855-1857 and 1869-1872 he served as state senator. He purchased Rancho de Cuati and adjacent land to develop his Lake Vineyard Ranch (now a large part of the city of San Marino), and with John S. Griffin purchased Rancho San Pascual, which has become the city of Pasadena. Wilson planted vineyards and citrus groves, and became active in business circles. He was the father of one son and three daughters, one of whom married James de Barth Shorb (q.v.), who became business manager of the ranch. Another married George Smith Patton (1856-1927) and became the mother of General George S. Patton, Jr., of World War II fame.

This is a significant collection. The correspondence is rich with the business affairs of the late nineteenth century. Documents concern business and social life in California (1850-1890); Indian affairs in Southern California (1852-1856); the wine industry; early history of Pasadena, San Marino, and Wilmington, California; the estate settlement of Solomon Sublette; and the Santa Fe trade. Legal topics of greatest interest are real property and agriculture.

Subject Headings:
Agriculture
Commercial Law
Estates
Municipalities
Real Property

WOLFSKILL, LEWIS (1848-1884)
1,622 pieces, 1830-1892; 1904-1946

Lewis Wolfskill, Southern California rancher and businessman, was the son of pioneer landowner, William Wolfskill, who had come to California from New Mexico in 1831 and married the daughter of early Californian Jose Ygnacio Lugo. Lewis Wolfskill married Luisa Dalton, daughter of Henry Dalton, another prominent early ranch owner in the Los Angeles area. He held extensive interests in ranching, mining, real estate, and other business ventures. In 1866 he inherited Rancho Santa Anita but sold it soon after. He conducted the affairs of Henry Dalton from 1873 to 1875 and managed the Centinela Orchard from 1873 to 1879.

This is a significant collection. The land and mining papers are extensive. Corporation and oil issues are the subject of late nineteenth-century and early twentieth-century documents. Other documents concern many California ranchos; mining in California (mainly San Bernardino) from 1864 to 1881, the Centinela Orchard, and legal papers pertaining to the litigation of Henry Dalton concerning squatters' claims; also the papers of Wolfskill's son Herbert (1906-1946) and of the Francisca (Wolfskill) Shepherd Estate (1904-1946). Other topics include negotiable instruments, insurance, water, taxation, and debtor and creditor relations.

Subject Headings:
Agriculture
Commercial Law
Contracts
Corporations
Debtor & Creditor
Estates
Insurance
Landlord & Tenant
Natural Resources
Real Property
Taxation
Water

WOLTER, CHARLES (1792-1856)
448 pieces, 1792; 1827-1970

Charles Wolter, ship captain and pioneer California land owner, was a native of Germany, who went to sea at the age of eighteen. He sought his fortune in the coastal shipping trade off the coast of South America and settled at Lima, Peru, for two years. He extended his business to Mazatlan, Mexico, and, as master of the ship "Lenore," came to Monterey, California, in about 1833. There he married Josefa Antonia (daughter of Jose Mariano Estrada), the widow of

Rafael Gomez, the first attorney general sent from Mexico City to California. Wolter adopted her five children, and they had five more of their own. He served as pilot for Commodore Stockton and the American forces during the Mexican War. Wolter invested in property in the city of Monterey and in Rancho Lupyomi in partnership with the artist Edward Vischer.

This collection is of marginal significance except for land papers in boxes 1 and 2. Documents concern land and business matters in early Monterey, California, Rancho Los Tularcitos, and Rancho El Toro.

Subject Headings:
Real Property
Title

WOODWORTH, SELIM E. (1815-1871)
approximately 1,600 pieces, 1834-1947

Selim E. Woodworth, Sr., United States naval officer and son of poet Samuel Woodworth, was born in New York City. In 1834, he sailed on a three-year cruise to the South Seas, and from 1838 to 1845 served in the United States Navy. He was sent across the continent in 1846 with an official message of the declaration of war with Mexico. Shortly after his arrival in San Francisco in the winter of 1847, he led the rescue of the Donner Party. Woodworth was elected to the California State Senate from Monterey in 1849, and soon after entered the commission business in San Francisco and became president of the First Vigilance Committee in 1851. Woodworth later re-entered the navy (from 1862 to 1867), serving as an officer in the United States fleet on the Mississippi River during the Civil War.

This is a moderately significant collection for the land and mining papers in boxes 1 and 4 particularly the mining papers for the Blue Wing Quartz Mine in Calaveras County, California, (1860-1864).

Subject Headings:
Commercial Law
Estates
Natural Resources
Real Property

WOOLWINE, THOMAS LEE (1874-1925)
approximately 600 pieces, 1914-1922

Thomas L. Woolwine, Los Angeles attorney, was a native of Tennessee. He received law degrees from Cumberland University in Tennessee in 1903 and from George Washington University in 1904. Woolwine, who came to California in 1896, was married to Alma Foy, the daughter of Samuel C. Foy, early Los Angeles businessman. Woolwine served in several capacities in Los Angeles city, county, and federal justice departments from 1897 to 1908. He was elected district attorney of Los Angeles for the years 1915-1923.

This is a significant collection in the area of municipal law and urban growth in the early twentieth century. Documents concern mainly Thomas L. Wollwine's term as Los Angeles city attorney; Los Angeles politics and Woolwine's campaign for governor of California in 1922.

Subject Headings:
Crimes
Law & Practice
Municipalities